Praise for "From *A*

"From Alpha to Zen is a thoug
which adds significantly to the canon.

Joy Maitland presents the reader with a thoughtful, considered and powerful argument for the Zen approach to leadership and her real-life experience of guiding leaders is evident. The book brings leadership guidance firmly into the 2020s, presenting a new way of seeing recent examples of leadership (both good and bad) as well as delivering unique perspectives on the leadership styles of historical figures. The book is a fascinating read, which provides a raft of practical tips and helps the reader to think anew about what true, lasting leadership is, and should be."

Lief Anya Schneider, Communications Director,
SBC London

"Congrats on putting this together. This book is thoughtful and challenging. Most of the exceptional leaders in your book are pretty fierce individuals when it comes to the wire. You put your points across with tact and a positive clarity that I remember only too well and took me back those few years ago when we first met. I struggle with the Higher Power, which ever form it may have, though you made the point very well when you offered, "If a vision is the destination, the higher power is the fuel.""

Antoine Kohler, Executive, GFG Alliance,
CEO, Marble Power Limited

"Joy Maitland's book is a treatise on modern leadership. It succinctly explains the difference between Alpha and Zen leadership and is extremely pragmatic in its conclusions. Joy is to be commended for writing a very readable book that piques the reader's interest with so many relevant and interesting anecdotes. This book will help any leader navigate through the complexities of 21st Century business management."

Stephen Grant, Executive Chairman, Cititec

"This is an impressive and timely book on leadership from Joy Maitland, that offers fresh insight on the topic. Joy hooks your attention from the first paragraph with her definition of Alpha and Zen leadership. Her book is a treasure trove of examples and compelling ideas that force us to reflect on our own styles of leadership in the 21st century, and determine where as leaders, change is necessary to be at our best, and inspire greatness in those we lead."

**Dr Sunday Popo-Ola, Associate Professor,
Imperial College London**

"From Alpha to Zen is a smart, interesting, and timely book. What Joy has produced is a compelling read that will inspire change in any leader. The book also includes interesting anecdotes from Joy's own life experiences as well as of leaders past and present, who were successful in their various fields. My favourite quote is: "Vision begins when one spots a gap and desires to fill it, for the greater good of many others. It is a selfless effort." Offering fresh insight on the important topic of leadership, this book is a must read."

Sharifa Sardal, EMEA Manager ET CSS

ABOUT THE AUTHOR

J oy Maitland is a multi-award-winning Executive Coach, Speaker and Author whose motto, "Be the Difference. Make the Difference", has served as her North Star in everything she does.

Joy has a wealth of senior-level corporate management experience, as well as a continued involvement with various organizations at Board level, which puts her in a unique position to help Executives advance their mission and gain greater success in their respective fields. She holds fellowships with the Institute of Directors (IoD), the Institute of Leadership and Management (TILM), and the Chartered Management Institute (CMI).

As an author, Joy empowers her readers to adopt modern leadership techniques as well as innovative ways of thinking and working in order to achieve leadership excellence. Her book "From Alpha to Zen: Leadership for a Brave New World" helps her growing worldwide readership in their journey to become the kind of leader who inspires those around them.

Joy is the Managing Director of Inemmo — a company focused on inspiring, empowering, and motivating business executives to build and expand their leadership capabilities to ensure future success through professional development, learning solutions, and executive coaching.

From Alpha to Zen

Leadership for a brave new world

By

Joy Maitland

This book is affectionally dedicated to...

My parents, Lessy and Cecil Maitland
I am because you were.
I love you.

*

My dear sister, Trudi and brother, Lincoln
You are the truest and purest forms of love.

*

My great friend and business partner, Atiya
Thank you for your unwavering support.

Table of Contents

INTRODUCTION

This is not the first book written on leadership, and it won't be the last. The aggressive trend of penning books and articles on this subject matter underscores two inescapable truisms. The first is that leadership remains a critical aspect of how man organizes society. The second is that in a rapidly evolving global society, radical changes are taking place at every level, demanding a clear shift in approach to modern leadership. Indeed, in some respects, a radical rethink of how modern man is led is the only sure way to remain on the cutting-edge of leadership in the twenty-first century.

Titled *From Alpha to Zen*, the issues this book seeks to dwell on revolve around the nature of leadership, nations, organizations, and companies in the world will adopt to make a maximum impact in the areas of their expertise. We are about to take a critical look at how influential leaders like Nelson Mandela, Bill Gates Jr., Margaret Thatcher, Oprah Winfrey, Jack Ma, Jacinda Arden, Elon Musk and other notable greats wielded their power to transform society – and the leadership styles they developed.

The United Kingdom – much like the rest of the world – has nurtured leaders worth emulating and others not as exemplarily gifted. There are specific characteristics and trends that stand out in the assessment of excellence in leadership, with which we do well to familiarize ourselves. These trends and characteristics define whether one's style fits in the category of Alpha or Zen leadership. This book aims to delve into the mindset and core philosophy that propelled influential leaders of the past to excel and steered modern leaders down that same path to greatness.

Many thought leaders have vigorously debated the dichotomy between born and made leaders. The operating assumption is that there are indeed leaders born to lead and others who emerged as a factor of being "made." This is a false dichotomy that this book will steer clear of – because there are no reliable studies that have proved, conclusively, that genetic predisposition has a role to play in the dynamism of leadership one eventually displays. Neither the Alpha nor the Zen leader was born to lead; they emerged as a result of demonstrable variables.

In this book, I take the view that great leaders emerge because of an innate desire to see others thrive. They connect with those they lead at a level so deep that these individuals, even without conscious thought, feel seen, understood, and valued. They willingly follow the empathetic leader because they have demonstrated an understanding of the *fundamental* need to treat those they lead as human beings. This trait is common in many Zen leaders.

Given the number of books on leadership already on the shelves, a critical reader might ask why the need for another. "What value does the new book, focused on Alpha or Zen leadership, add?", they might doubtingly ask. That is a great question. This book proposes to act as a bridge between the leadership paradigms of the past and the present. It will launch us into the curious orbit of behavior, philosophy, and drive that a modern leader needs to spin in to lead with admirable excellence.

The examples of leaders allowed to grace the pages of this book are those whose actions and words have had either a powerful impact or grimly affected those they led. There can be no exemplary leadership without poor leadership for comparison. There can be no *Zen* without *Alpha*. The dominant traits highlighted in this narrative are those exemplified in winners – men and women with leadership anchored in a Zen leadership style.

The issues raised in this discussion are profound and urgent, but they must begin in the right place. No leader can become successful until they are bitten by the bug of vision – a precise painting of the kind of world they want to emerge. The drive to create that world will be directly proportionate to the vision's clarity and the projectable impact on those to benefit from it.

Therefore, the most credible way to begin this discussion is to delve into a refreshing review of vision. We want to consider what vision truly is, how it affects goals, objectives, and the culture within an establishment – and how it must guide each aspect of operations to move a company in the general direction of the ultimate picture. More importantly, I want to showcase the different and typical approaches adopted by an Alpha leader and a Zen leader and the *outcome* of applying the two different styles.

As you think about leadership, you have undoubtedly considered the notion that a great leader must remain relevant to succeed. Have you ever asked why many seasoned leaders have failed at remaining relevant? Have you ever wondered why failing to keep on the cutting-edge of trends in leadership has undone many promising careers?

Providing a *clear* understanding of prevailing trends in leadership is the goal of this book. I also aim to help the world mold leaders whose relevance and endurance will create an atmosphere where an individual's full potential is enabled for the good of all.

Therefore, as we tackle the issue of vision, the question I want you to keep at the back of your mind is – *can anyone paint a better picture of the world than we have now?* With the technological breakthroughs in medicine, the aggressive exploration of space and marine life, the technological advancements in all spheres of life, what is left to imagine? Can one still have a vision of a better world than this? Is a Zen leader the answer, or should the world remain in the throes of Alpha leadership to forge ahead?

I'm about to open your eyes, wherever you are in the world, to the reason a vision is not only critical but is a must to move you and those around you to a more promising reality.

Leadership, you are about to discover, is more about solving societal problems than earning personal glory at fellow humans' expense. If you conclude that Zen leadership suits the twenty-first century far better than Alpha leadership by the end of this book, I would have achieved my goal.

CHAPTER 1

THE ULTIMATE PICTURE

Vision has been described in several ways by notable players in related fields. They talk about empires of the mind, a promise, an aspiration, seeing the invisible, seeing the possibilities, and even a guiding light. The common thread in these definitions is an imagined place or a standard of excellence where all efforts need to be focused on achieving the desired outcome.

I agree with the notion that part of the definition of vision includes a rewarding outcome. However, I believe that vision is far broader than that. Vision is not only about the result but the journey to get there. Moreover, vision provides the *motivation*, the "why," without which there is no drive, energy, or will to act.

From the outset, it is essential to mention that a vision without execution is simply a dream, a reason why, for many, their visions are left unfulfilled. That's why a reading of many vision statements portray a sense of an ongoing quest or journey. Circumstances can change rapidly and may affect both the direction, speed, and ability of the key players to keep the ship on the path to achieve the desired vision. Despite all, those who achieve it understand that our vision often calls us to be more than we currently are and to trust that we have an innate aptitude for greatness.

In using the example of former South African President, Nelson Mandela, I want us to look at how a Zen leader, guided by the highest moral standards, would handle the matter of vision. In him, I want us to understand how a Zen mindset moves one from having a vision to moving the masses along its roadmap.

The Mandela Example

Adoring fans in South Africa called him Madiba or *Tata Mkulu* – Grandpa. The lanky, driven boy was born in the village of Mvezo, in Eastern Cape, in 1918. Born Rolihlahla Mandela, he grew up on the banks of the Mbashe River, in Transkei, in what he thought was a wonderful land, blessed with vast farmlands, lovely people, and some of the most inviting mountains, plains, and rivers the world has ever known. In his youth, he believed he would lead a normal life in his native land. He was going to grow up content like the other children.

As Mandela graduated from adolescence to adulthood, he became troubled by what he judged rightly to be an *unjust* system of governance, which relegated black people to a second-class status and was propped up by a brutal police force. Dubbed apartheid, the racist Afrikaners crafted a lifestyle that availed to them all the instruments of power – the police, the military, the economy, excellent schools, and farmlands. All the nation's major groups were subjected to a life in the shanties of Soweto and slums of Pretoria – and many others to slavery in the farmlands and the goldmines. Life was hopeless in the land.

Nelson Mandela was disturbed by what he saw as an affront to the dignity of his people. He was so troubled by the situation that he felt compelled to do something about it. He was not deterred by his assessment that doing anything about apartheid would come with the danger of facing off with security forces, an entrenched system of brutality, and the despair of his people.

In it all, Mandela was guided by the powerful *vision* of a nation where all the communities in the land lived in harmony and shared its prosperity. In his mind, the young man imagined a South Africa where the blacks, the whites, and the coloreds went to school together, attended church services together, lived in the same neighborhoods, and saw in each South African a fellow citizen. That kind of thoughtfulness, you will later realize, is the building block that underpins Zen leadership.

That vision, though, was hotly opposed by Boers, who sought to retain their privileged status in the nation and were prepared to maintain the status quo through *state-sponsored* violence. It was enough to make anyone without a vision buckle under the weight of fear and just let it be. Mandela, though, was so sold on the power of his vision that bullets and state terror were not going to cower him – he was not in it for self; he was in it for a nation. As you can already tell, the Boers were led by an *Alpha complex* that gave way to Alpha leadership.

Toward the lofty goal of liberating his motherland, a young Nelson enrolled in law school, became a member of the African National Congress, and was instrumental in founding the armed wing of the party – uMkhonto we Sizwe. Mandela was later arrested and was jailed for twenty-seven years, with hard labor, on Robben Island. Upon his release, he led the nation to independence, becoming the first President of an independent South Africa. During that presidency, his vision, anchored in the *thoughtfulness* of liberating a nation and setting it on a path to prosperity for all, found grace in the core tenets of Zen leadership – a calm, all-inclusive and participative governance.

The Jacinda Ardern Example

Jacinda Ardern, the 40th prime minister of New Zealand, currently serving her second term in office, has been described as "a leader for our times." Born in 1980, she is the youngest female Prime Minister that New Zealand, a country of just under five million people, has ever had and has already made quite an impact on the world of Politics. Since becoming Prime Minister, she has frequently been praised for her optimism, decisiveness, approachability, determination, authenticity, and empathy.

She has been applauded for her government's response to the Coronavirus pandemic, having acted decisively with an early lockdown that essentially all but eliminated the spread of the virus, helping New Zealand avoid the massive spread of infections and the many deaths that have ravaged the US and Europe.

On March 15th, 2019, fifty-one people died when a lone gunman mounted a terrorist attack during Friday Prayer, on two mosques in Christchurch. Just thirty-six hours later, Jacinda Arden had acted and robustly mobilised politicians to tighten up gun laws. On March 21st, she announced a sweeping ban of assault rifles and military-style semi-automatics. Jacinda went further and called for a global fight to root out racist right-wing ideology and ensure that we do not create an environment in which it can flourish.

Jacinda Arden's 2030 vision realized, would see the end of child poverty in New Zealand with no health inequalities based on race, wealth, or region. She places emphasis on kindness and empathy.

"I think one of the sad things that I've seen in political leadership is – because we've placed over time so much emphasis on notions of assertiveness and strength – that we probably have assumed that it means you can't have those other qualities of kindness and empathy. And yet, when you think about all the big challenges that we face in the world, that's probably the quality we need the most."

The Branson Example

Sir. Richard Branson was born Richard Charles Nicholas Branson, in Blackheath, London, on July 18, 1950, to a former ballet dancer named Eve. His father was a barrister by the name Edward James Branson. His grandfather, Sir George Arthur Harwin Branson, was a judge of the High Court of Justice and a Privy Councillor.

Branson was educated at Scaitcliffe School, a prep school in Surrey, before briefly attending Cliff View House School in Sussex. He attended Steve School, an independent school in Buckinghamshire, until the age of sixteen.

Branson has had dyslexia and poor academic performance. On his last day at school, his tepid headmaster,

Robert Drayson, told him he would go on to either end up in prison or become a millionaire. With his parents' support, he became a millionaire and has become a business magnate, investor, and author.

Starting as an entrepreneur at the early age of sixteen, Richard founded a magazine called *Student* and later founded Virgin Records. He was accused of selling records without paying taxes and was made to pay 70,000.00 pounds in a settlement that saw his parents remortgage their family home to meet the need. Not to be deterred, he founded the Virgin Group in 1970, the parent company under which sit four hundred companies, in various fields, within the business world.

Having ventured into the airline industry with his Virgin Atlantic fleet, Branson would later partner with Microsoft co-founder Paul Allen and engineer Burt Rutan to plot space exploration through Virgin Galactic and the space shuttle, SpaceShip Two. Sir Richard Branson has emerged as one of the world's most innovative and futuristic leaders. He has used his enormous wealth to solve issues that have limited man's ability to explore the universe and make its elements work for all humanity's good.

That the failure of his Virgin Cola, Virgin Clothing, Virgin Cars, Virgin Publishing, and Brides has not dampened his spirit to invest aggressively is what we must take away from his vision of giving the world a habitation without limits.

We can all strive to overcome incredible odds and manage failure, so failure does not end a dream but spark it instead.

Discontentment

The inspiring life of Nelson Mandela is a perfect illustration of the power of vision. Before there is a vision, there will be *discontentment* with the current situation. Whether in a political, academic, church, business, or a diplomatic setting, a superior vision is only possible when one is discontented with the prevailing circumstances.

So strong must that discontentment be that they who are afflicted with it are spurred to action to cause change. They must feel strongly about the matter enough to be willing to invest time and energy, and resources in the drive to force change. In South Africa, Mandela was so persuaded about a unified South Africa vision that he was willing to die in its pursuit. In Britain, Sir Richard Branson was so taken with his vision of an airline that offered a certain quality of experience in the air that he was willing to invest money and time in its pursuit. In New Zealand, Jacinda Arden's steely commitment to politics devoid of isolationism and national self-interest, supports her vision of a better world, that provides a refuge for those who need it. Vision begins when one spots a gap and desires to fill it for the greater good of many others. It is a selfless effort.

Discontentment alone, however, will not amount to anything; it must be followed with a coherent thought process:

a. Sure, I am not satisfied with the way things are, but is there anything I can realistically do to effect meaningful change?

b. What will it take in sweat, time, resources, and relations to effect change? Will it be worth the inevitable sacrifice?

c. How long will it take to move from where things currently stand to where I want them to be? Will it be within my lifetime, or am I starting a process that will outlive me?

Those are important questions to ask. Both a Zen and an Alpha leader will ask them. The difference is in how they will approach achieving the vision once they start the process. The Alpha leader will bulldoze everyone into cowardly going along with his or her whims. The Zen leader will thoughtfully bring subjects along through persuasion, consultation, and reliance on data, analysis, and science. An Alpha leader's authoritarian nature might move things along faster in the initial stages of rolling out a vision, but in the end, the path turns dark. A Zen leader will start much slower, but in the end, their vision will catch fire, and those they lead will buy into the vision and become aware of its eventual benefits for all.

There are thought leaders who have argued that vision is about creating something from nothing. I guess there's a way one might view it as such, but I think the better way is to view vision as a process made possible because of the failure of existing structures to comprehensively and conclusively address people's needs. It is the gap left by the failure that sparks one's discontentment and gives way to a strong desire for change.

Thus, discontent is only helpful and positive if it leads to an evaluation of what one is ready and able to do – and acts as the catalyst for the birth of a vision. It is, thus, the mother of a vision.

Leadership

It took Nelson Mandela to liberate South Africa and set the nation on a path to his vision. It took Sir Richard Branson to found Virgin Atlantic and set the airline on a path to dominance in the air. It took Elon Musk, an industrial designer and engineer, to found SpaceX. Elon has been described as a Renaissance man of this era. The imaginer of an empire (a vision) must take charge of leading people toward the greatness of that vision. They will act as the captain or pilot who will guide the ship toward the majesty imagined in his or her mind. How they lead people to that point determines if they are an Alpha or Zen leader.

Many companies have struggled and faltered in the drive toward maximum productivity and on the path to their vision because they have put at the helm men or women not committed to the entity's vision. Some have left at the helm leaders whose style is authoritarian, whose philosophy is built upon a foundation of *my way or the highway*, and whose sole gratification is ultimate glory for self. It is critical that the person who created the vision be cast at the helm and given the time, resources, and full cooperation to achieve the desired vision and be held accountable for the pace and quality of results realized along the way.

In any company, effective leadership is a product of a deep understanding of vision – and a fiery commitment to it. There must be a strong sense of the positive impact the vision will have on people. There must be a powerful sense of the values, culture, and identity necessary to develop a new reality among the people.

Therefore, discontent needs to urge in one the willingness to lead a group of people toward a new reality or vision. A leader who lacks a commitment to the vision will inevitably crash the ship on an iceberg. They will eventually surrender to the temptation to quit when the tide is strong; because of a lack of commitment to the vision's power.

It is not an assertion without evidence to declare that the men and women the world has adored as great leaders have been those who established their companies in the strong roots of a powerful and realistic vision. They have capably and persuasively communicated the pathway and nature of the product to be availed to the world because of adherence to the vision. They have *painted* an inspiring picture of the kind of world that is possible and helped all those around them look forward to that outcome.

The men and women described above have diligently applied Zen rather than Alpha leadership skills to achieve their vision. Whether one talks about Elon Musk, Jack Ma, Jeff Bezos, Oprah Winfrey, Margaret Thatcher, or Winston Churchill, what stands out is the fact that the vision endured and survived the winds of time. Compare that to the vision authoritarians like Adolf Hitler, Pol Pot, and Idi Amin Dada dreamed up. Where are their visions now? Hitler's Aryan Nation collapsed. Pol Pot's Cambodia has become a democracy. Amin Dada's Uganda has struggled and is currently experimenting with democracy, too. In a word, a vision subjected to Alpha leadership will eventually come to one conclusion – *failure*.

The Inemmo Experience

Before I conclude this chapter, I feel compelled to tell the story of my leadership journey and the creation of the leadership and development consultancy known by the musical acronym, Inemmo. **In**Em**M**o stands for Inspire, Empower, and Motivate.

I have read extensively on the twin subjects of psychology and philosophy. My goal was to have a clearer view of the motivating factors and what makes us who we are as individuals.

Of the books I read, Stephen R. Covey's *The Seven Habits of Highly Effective People* won the race to calm my itch. It became my guide to shape myself into a formidable player in the field of mentorship and overall consultancy. I wrote programmes based on the book's core philosophy. I watched as Inemmo gradually morphed into a consultancy focused on identifying and nurturing greatness in the clients with whom we have had the pleasure of working.

My vision was to create a world where companies grew based on greatness urged out of workers and mid-level managers. When I became a manager and was suddenly responsible for groups of individuals, a painful truth soon grew clear to me – that many companies put little investment into developing the true potential of those lower down the pecking order. They invest heavily at the top on leadership development but far less at the bottom or middle, where the need could very well be much more significant. They then would wonder why their employees are disengaged and disruptive.

I found this approach was concerning because I had always believed that, as a manager, one should look to lead by example, with the sole aim that colleagues would be inspired to realize their potential – no matter where in the office ranking, they stood. That was my vision going in and has remained my guide as I have coached many people around the world to identify and maximize their potential. Of course, I must admit that going in, I did not know a thing about either Alpha or Zen leadership. Several years in, I appreciate the role vision plays in leadership and understand the significant role the Zen approach plays in giving the vision a firm foundation to stand on.

These three Zen examples I have presented before you – South Africa, Virgin Atlantic, and Inemmo – are meant to help you appreciate that a vision is not necessarily a factor of huge enterprise only; most times, it is a factor of rather small ones. Indeed, my experience at Inemmo points to the reality that leadership potential lies in each of us and can be identified to be nurtured to better society.

Sacrifice

The term I like better than sacrifice is selflessness. We have established that vision is only relevant if it is acted upon. The one who must get it going is the man or the woman who created the vision. This calls for sacrifice on a scale matched only by the amount of pressure, demands, and the timeframe it will take to set the ship on the path to where it needs to sail. There are three critical areas in which one will need to sacrifice heavily:

a. Family. Taking that first step in leading the way toward a new reality demands time and dedication. In many instances, that time will be *borrowed* from the family and other core needs if only to establish the new venture on a foundation firm enough to launch it successfully. Care must be taken to ensure that a balance is struck that keeps the family and the vision into their right perspectives.

b. Resources. Many banks and other lenders are willing to fund promising startups. There are individuals wealthy and investment-oriented enough to fund ideas they assess as winners if well supported. However, it remains a truism that as one gets down to building a foundation for his or her vision, there will be the need to deploy personal resources in time, money, energy, and intellectual giftedness to succeed.

c. Pleasures. Digging deep roots for a vision is a demanding experience. One needs to let go of pleasures to focus on the vision. Often, not much time will be available for friends and socializing in general. Laying a deep foundation for a vision is a lonely and unnerving exercise. The only motivating factor is the projected benefit of the vision on the lives of the people it is targeted to impact.

A vision, however small, is not to be taken lightly; it is always daunting. One needs to have a strong foundation in character, fortitude, and the grace it takes to set off on a journey that may not be easy to explain to others. For example, why did Mandela feel so strongly about liberation? Why did Branson find it necessary for a new way to fly to be introduced in the skies? Why did I feel strongly about empowering workers to become a far greater version of themselves? Yes, it can be unnerving, but I have found that your courage will expand in line with your vision if you allow it.

In the next chapter, I want us to explore the role a higher power plays in planting fortitude in the one who has dared to have a vision. I hold it to be true that without the inspiration drawn from a power mightier than the visionary, a vision may never see the light of day – due to fear and discouragement. You will also sense that a Zen leader is more open to the influencing of a higher power than an Alpha leader – because the latter relies heavily on *self* while the former understand vulnerabilities.

CHAPTER 2

HIGHER POWER

Never one to follow in the footsteps of anyone blindly, I was not going to buy into the belief patterns of family or of any system whose background I did not dig deeply into to understand better. I wanted my life to be tied to a force that inspired greatness in me because it lent itself to the firm foundation of a coherent and sustainable philosophy of life.

As an immigrant to the UK, that became such an important matter because the sense of dislocation from ancestral roots can be overwhelming. It gets even trickier when departure from those roots is guided by the powerful need to make something of one's life. In a vast world where man is reduced to but a speck on a globe, it is necessary to look to a force with the ability to infuse courage, grace, and inspiration in the critical moments of life.

Before I describe what a higher power is, let me pose the question – what do you think gave a boy like Mandela, born in Transkei, the courage to face a brutal system? What inspired him? What gave me the courage to embark on the journey to find a place where my core talents would have meaning? What inspired Sir Branson to imagine an airline of the scope of Virgin Atlantic? Indeed, vision played a critical role, but beyond vision, there had to have been a force that urged Mandela and Branson, and me to stop resting on our laurels and get out to change the world. That steadying force in one's life is what I call a higher power.

Before I delve deeper into this matter, I remind us of this book's title and theme – *From Alpha to Zen*. In this chapter's discussion, I want us to pay attention to the nature of the forces that have been a shaper of *philosophy* and have provided *inspiration* to the two types of leaders we have defined. For example, what force inspired Jack Ma to leave his native China and get fixated on the need to open up China through technology?

The Jack Ma Example

The future business magnate and ambassador for Chinese business was born in Zhengzhou, China, in 1964. A young Jack started learning English by steadily conversing with English-speakers at the Zhengzhou International Hotel. He rode more than seventeen kilometers to the hotel to play a guide to the tourists so that he could learn English.

During his tours, a young Jack linked up with a pen pal, who, finding it hard to pronounce his native name, nicknamed him Jack – the name stuck. It was the name that would later serve him well when he arrived in the United States of America and began to lead a life of innovation, working with others to connect China to the information superhighway.

Before going to the USA, however, Ma sat for his university entrance exams three times. He then went to the Zhengzhou Teachers Institute and graduated in 1988 with a Bachelor of Arts in English and later taught at the Hangzhou Dianzi University. Amazingly, Jack applied ten times to the Harvard Business School and was rejected all ten times.

In 1995, Jack Ma went to the USA with his friends and started the string of internet companies that would eventually lead him to think more broadly about the opportunities the internet presented. He never looked back. At one point, a business venture made more than eight hundred thousand dollars. Not surprisingly, when it was time to think even bigger, together with his friend, he co-founded Alibaba, which was later to become a global conglomerate. Ma was on his way to becoming a *dominant* player in international commerce.

Asked about the force that has guided his life, Jack has been quick to mention Buddhism and Taoism as the philosophical cornerstones of his life. The notion that suffering can be overcome by attaining Nirvana is at the center of his beliefs. Therefore, his higher power is the belief in the way of life that will eventually end suffering in the world. Taoism and Buddhism have presented this innovator with an organizing philosophy that keeps him focused and charged up in moments when life's challenges appear overwhelming and discouraging.

We have already noted that a Zen leader acts for the good of all, not just for his or her own good like the Alpha leader does. In Ma's life, what you see is a man whose philosophy of life, *the eradication of suffering*, was going to mold him into a thoughtful leader – Zen leadership. He was going to develop into a leader whose manner and bearing emanated from a place of empathy and the desire to alleviate pain, not propagate it. But before we get to that foundational matter, let us define what a higher power is.

Defining Higher Power

You have undoubtedly interacted with various and pithier definitions of a higher power. There will be those who instantly think about God when we talk of a higher power. I do not begrudge them if that is what it means to them. In my search for a force to ally my sensibilities with, however, I realized that a higher power is not necessarily a deity; it can be any number of forces that allow you to, for the first time, truly realize the greatness in you.

   a.   A spiritually-based positive attitude. I am positive in my conscious mind because I am assured that all the forces and powers of the universe work for my good each day. What I came to regard as the higher power in my life helped me organize my life around a coherent philosophy that guides how I relate to others and operate in the world and that I can rely on whenever I need inspiration. I am certain many people are similarly wired to turn to a core philosophy as the power they surrender to for courage and inspiration and marching orders. What inevitably follows is the realization of greater success, happiness, and fulfillment.

b. God. I have already alluded to the fact that a deity is one of the forces one may turn to for courage and inspiration. At the end of the day, though, you will discover that *belief* in the power of God is just another way to organize one's life. It is also a philosophy of life. It would be challenging to have faith in God if you did not believe in his existence. If belief in that force provides much-needed inspiration to face the multiplicity of challenges life offers, why not?

c. Serendipity. In 1928, Sir Alexander Fleming, a Scottish researcher, returned from a vacation to find an odd-looking mold developed on an uncovered petri dish. He isolated the mold and identified it as the Penicillium genus. According to published reports, Fleming said, "One sometimes finds what one is not looking for. When I woke up just after dawn on Sept. 28, 1928, I certainly didn't plan to revolutionize all medicine by discovering the world's first antibiotic or bacteria killer. But I guess that was exactly what I did." Seeing this as a happy accident is not to see the whole picture; indeed, serendipity requires perseverance, preparation, and opportunity. The French philosopher Sylvie Catellin proposed that serendipity is a *"fundamental disposition of human beings in the process of discovery."*

I am aware that the ancient Himalayan tribes – and fierce tribal groups in South America and Africa – have found inspiration in a system of cosmic divinities around which they have created a fitting philosophy of life. In the realm of invention, war, worship, conquest, and exploration, these groups of people have relied on the said divinities to keep on the path to greatness – to unhindered exploits.

I glean from this understanding of a higher power is the inbuilt need of man to have a form of force greater than self. We all need the assurance that there is a force looking out for us – cheering us on in this uncertain world. We recognize, thus, the notion that the force is mightier and can steer our thoughts in the desired direction. The role of the force is to make us better. Had Jack Ma never weaved his life's theme around the powerful Buddhist philosophy that suffering can be ended, he probably would have never founded the global

Jack Ma Foundation. This foundation has become a leading philanthropic outfit focused on education and health issues. He also founded the Hupan School to train the next generation of Chinese business leaders. That is what reliance on a higher power does to one with focus and determination.

Once again, note that Ma's focus – because of the higher power he surrendered to – predisposed him to be his brother's keeper. It molded out of him a natural Zen leader. His life was about helping the suffering – alleviating pain and poverty. That is in stark contrast to an Alpha leader like Hitler, whose sole goal was to create an empire that gratified his twisted psychological thrill to dominate the world.

The next important fact to glean is the infallibility of man. In recognition of our finiteness, we seek to ally with a force more powerful than us to help us succeed where we would be sure to fail. Reliance on a higher power gives us that additional element we need to carry on even when it all looks dire and hopeless. It provides us the courage to make just one more step when we would rather fold up and call it quits, hiding behind the false satisfaction that *at least I gave it my best shot.*

Perhaps Sir Mohammed Anwar Pervez OBE, HPk founder of Bestway Group, said it best.

"At the heart of Bestway Group's philosophy is the desire to help those less fortunate than others by supporting charities and empowering communities in the United Kingdom and Pakistan.

It is my article of *faith* that Bestway Group companies and charitable trusts embody the highest standards of corporate social responsibility by supporting local communities and stakeholders that have contributed towards the success of the businesses."

Regardless of how one has become a leader, the twenty-first century demands that a *continuous* evaluation and sharpening of core skills remain a priority to keep a leader on a path to relevance and eventual success. Despite the incredible challenges many leaders have faced, they have stayed the course. What is it that keeps them going? It is the inspiration drawn from a higher power.

Where there is a clear vision, there *must* be a higher power. If a vision is the destination, a higher power is the fuel one needs to get there. It is the encouragement one needs to stay focused when the going gets tough, as it always inevitably does. It is the silent voice that whispers in the ear that all will end well if you hang in there – for just a second, a minute, an hour, a day, a month, a year longer!

This is the point at which I proposed to make a profound statement about the title of this book. *From Alpha to Zen* contemplates a twenty-first-century world where leaders are guided away from the Alpha approach of authoritarianism to the Zen approach of inclusivity, thoughtfulness, empathy, and reliance on facts and data to lead.

This brave new century has revealed its character early. It has shown its stripes as those defined by the need for global cohesiveness, the rule of law, and human togetherness – built upon a foundation of trade treaties, international bodies, and bilateral and multilateral engagements. Under this scenario, isn't it evident that only a thoughtful, exposed, and inspired leader can survive and even prosper? That is what Zen leadership is about. An Alpha leader will soon find the global commerce terrain too nuanced and too complicated to fathom. Global progress triggers decay for an Alpha leader!

A Leader's Higher Power

I am yet to meet a leader who does not surrender to the might of a higher power in leadership. In the twenty-first century, we live in a world where the changes we encounter are rapid, profound, and in many cases, unprecedented. Whether in the realm of space exploration, medical breakthroughs with attendant ethical issues, marine biology, or nuclear technology, the times are perilous, and leaders must have the fortitude of character to lead at all.

Finding fortitude in Jehovah as his higher power, President George W. Bush was spotted in the Rose Garden walking alone, deep in thought, moments before he launched the Iraq war, which would later dislodge Saddam Hussein from power. When he was asked what had been on his mind – as he had taken that lonely walk in the famous garden – he said he had been talking to his Maker.

The self-proclaimed agnostic Elon Musk says he puts his faith in science, how the laws of the universe work, and in humankind. Still, in August 2020, after the historic SpaceX splashdown, the first by US astronauts in 45 years, he told reporters, "I'm not very religious, but I prayed for this one."

The evening Nelson Mandela walked out of the jailhouse that had trapped him under inhumane conditions for twenty-seven dreary years, he felt the sting of tears and made a resolution. *If I don't leave my bitterness behind, I will still be in this very prison.* He left the bitterness at the prison door and instead found fortitude in a higher power – the vision of a free and prosperous South Africa.

Great leaders have that one thing in common – a higher power that keeps them *grounded* and *focused* on the mission. They have surrendered to the fact that they are human and need a power greater than themselves. Indeed, those who have failed to view themselves as human have gone on to evolve into dangerous dictators. Leaders like Amin Dada of Uganda, Pol Pot of Cambodia, Mobutu Sese Seko of Congo, and a myriad of other South American despots wore their Alpha mantra like a medal.

Be it in the corporate, church, academia, or military realm, there must be a sense of human self-doubt and fallibility for one to be great. Such self-doubt leads to the need to rely on a power outside the abilities one believes they possess and sets them on a path to partnership with a superior *force* — a force that makes them better. Again, we are deep into Zen leadership territory here.

Therefore, the question I hear you ask is — does it mean a leader without a higher power cannot go on to succeed in leadership? Does an Alpha leader, fully reliant on chest-thumping, stand a chance at success at all? The answer is no; it is impossible to succeed without a higher power in either the Alpha or Zen-style leadership. It is impossible to find the courage, inspiration, and grace one needs to remain doggedly focused without being spurred on by a power beyond one's abilities.

Earlier, I told you that a critical understanding of psychology and philosophy have helped me shape a desired higher power in my life. I have a way of looking at life that helps me organize my life in the only way I feel makes sense. In my consultancy, and in the manner I handle clients, the drive is to reach deep within each client and draw out the essential them and make that person a far better version of their current self. The primitive form in each of us, which naturally predisposes us to authoritarian Alpha-type automatons, is the dark spot Inemmo seeks to shine a bright light on so that a Zen-type predisposition emerges.

Therefore, my higher power is a philosophy at whose core is the belief that each of us is born to *emerge* into a Zen leader – a thoughtful, reasoned human being able to guide others toward a better outcome in their lives and society. That is a radical statement to make, and I understand that. I also appreciate its assertion that most of us fail to emerge into thoughtful leaders because the world has denied us the opportunity to lead. We have failed many people by not availing them the opportunity to explore their full potential. Still, it is not true that their primordial nature, which is the spark for Alpha tendencies, can't be overcome by digging out our better angels.

I am not one big with sentimentalism; I tend to be practical about life. I have, however, been woken up to the reality that success causes enormous joy in me. My joy is in seeing the young discover their abilities early so that they may play a meaningful role in society. By creating structured avenues through which they are guided to view themselves as emerging leaders, I draw satisfaction because my higher power has enabled me to touch another life and positively impact it.

A Dark Power

It would be a disservice to end this chapter without talking about the contrast. Where there is a higher power, there inevitably is a dark power. The world has witnessed the destruction of such *dark powers* as well. In Rwanda, for example, the world watched in horror as more than one million people were killed following the dramatic downing of a plane that killed President Juvenal Habyarimana. In a sad attempt to ethnically cleanse a nation, a dark power seized misguided generals to cause mayhem.

In the emerging *theme* of this book, you can already tell that authoritarian, Alpha leadership is equated to darkness while participative inclusivity is viewed as anchored on the grace of a higher power. Alpha leadership, because of its corrosive and destructive impact, has slowly faded off the world stage. However, we still see it in places like North Korea and some African nations, where an amalgamation of Alpha leaders and a limited form of Zen leadership are brought to bear to create a false sense of inclusivity.

With stunning regularity, the world had witnessed the dark powers at play – Hitler in Germany, Pol Pot in Cambodia, Nkurunziza in Burundi. It is also arguable that the vociferous global forces driving a xenophobic agenda are led by characters who bow to the whims of a *dark power* – not a higher power. The power calling the shots in their lives is a dark, destructive force that inspires only fear, death, and unrest rather than human betterment.

It says something shockingly challenging about human nature that even those who bow to a dark power can emerge into powerful leaders for their diabolical causes. Why do people follow darkness when the path to light and progress seems so clear and so beneficial? Why do corporations pay their workers pitifully when profit margins read so high? Why do military officials prepare for war when a bit of diplomacy can save lives? Why do churches fail to speak forcefully for the ideals they espouse when a leader they support is in power?

The answer to those probing questions is one – it is about self-preservation, driven purely by a dark power. It is that dark power that activates the need to compromise on principles, bend the rules a tad, look the other way, become a despot, and even engage in double standards when convenient. Maybe such darkness is best illustrated by what happened in the United States of America, where President Donald Trump, despite just two months left to a general election, pompously nominated Judge Amy Coney Barrett, of the US Court of Appeals for the Seventh Circuit, to the US Supreme Court to replace the late Justice Ruth Bader Ginsburg. It was a classic example of Alpha leadership.

Faced with a strikingly similar situation four years ago, President Barack Obama nominated Judge Merrick Garland – nine months to the general election. Republicans bulked, citing the need to let the next President appoint a judge. They, thus, declined to vote on the nomination. Suddenly, the very same Republicans were willing to have Judge Amy seated on the bench a month to an election in defiance of a position they had taken with Obama.

Some will call that smartness. Others will call it politics. I view it as a dark path and lack of qualms about the moral relativism evidencing in leadership today. Where there is a higher power, leadership will inevitably evolve around principles. A higher power holds leaders accountable to conscience. It goads one to shun moral relativism, convenience and to act only in accordance with rightness.

Let me close this segment by making this pertinent statement about the two powers – dark and higher. A higher power generates in leaders the ability to positively impact lives for a long, long time. A dark power quickly burns itself out and leaves people in a state of devastation, turmoil, and with questions about human nature. If a leader uplifts society, they are guided by a higher power; if they are stalked by death and mayhem, they are inspired by a dark power – like was the case with Hitler.

As leaders today – called to shape destinies at a time the world is changing in profound ways – we do well to search deep within ourselves the power that we respond to when we think about life. Make that power your *ally* in the drive toward your vision because it will inevitably get tough. You will need the reassurance of a force outside yourself. You will seek the whisper of a still voice that says, *despite the grim setbacks, it will turn out just fine.* A Zen leader can relate to that higher power because of his or her character of meekness and deep introspection; an Alpha leader views meekness as a failure and is, thus, unable to tap into that well of inspiration.

In the next chapter, we shift our attention to one of the most critical elements in leadership. I call it character – or personality. How does it shape Zen leadership? How does it affect Alpha leadership? We are about to explore the role it plays in shaping leadership and predisposing one to success or failure.

CHAPTER 3

CHARACTER

The issues we have tackled in the first two chapters have been rather weighty ones. Vision and a Higher Power are at the base or foundation of leadership. They determine whether or not a leader will succeed in achieving their intended goals. Getting a vision right is, thus, the first step. The second is to ally with a force that will keep you inspired as you navigate the journey – for it is, indeed, a journey, not a destination. Hence, even when we may, on occasion, appear to have failed, the truth may be that we are simply being called to take another route—a route that may result in a more favorable outcome, one far beyond our expectations. The third, which we need to focus on in this chapter, is character or the moral fiber of a leader.

At the core of the supposition that a leader is one whose character is a winner is the belief that those they lead respond to evidence of integrity in the leader. It is the integrity demonstrated by a leader that attracts loyalty and confidence in their actions and the path chosen toward success.

I have concluded that the matter of character cannot be dealt with as a nice-to-have. I have realized that it is the definer of the nature of leadership one has to offer. If vision is a picture of what is possible and a higher power is the driving force that provides the impetus, power, or energy, then one's character is their north star, the guiding light that shines from within and without. This quote by Warren Buffett, an American business magnate and investor, nicely encapsulates my own beliefs around the subject of character:

"Somebody once said that in looking for people to hire, you look for three qualities: integrity, intelligence, and energy. And if you don't have the first, the other two will kill you. You think about it; it's true. If you hire somebody without integrity, you really want them to be dumb and lazy."

Defining Character

Many see character as something measurable. In essence, character, to me, is who we really are, away from the regulations that demand a certain kind of behavior. In other words, left to your own devices, who are you? What makes you tick? After all the layers have been peeled off, who are you at your core? That's what character is to me – that undiluted you!

In leadership, the character one brings to the table shapes the way subjects respond to his or her style and nature of temperament evidenced. In the city of Calcutta, India, the diminutive Albanian nun, Mother Teresa, was known as a caring, loving nun because of her character of *love*. Each waking hour was dedicated to finding new ways of reaching out to the destitute and broken on the streets.

Due to her abiding love, if one walked up to any of the impoverished street dwellers in Calcutta and asked who Mother Teresa was, the answer would be one of adoration and respect – she was kind and loving and humble. Those words would be attributed to a much deeper sense of who Mother Teresa was. At the core of those descriptive words is character not just formed in life but tried and tested over a long period of time by life's fierce storms. She often said, "I will never attend an anti-war rally; if you have a peace rally, invite me."

Like Mother Teresa and Prime Minister Margaret Thatcher, and the corporate leaders I have alluded to already, character is critical to success. It is the motivator. It is the assurance. It is the reason one can give as the reason for following a leader. Thus, it remains at the core of leadership as, perhaps, one of the most critical factors – along with vision and dependence on a higher power. It does decide whether the sail to the destination will be a smooth or a rough one – pegged purely on the personality of the man or woman at the helm.

In my readings – and based on my observation of leaders in politics, the corporate world, and in the church circles – I have come up with what I view as the core character traits that have been evident in successful leaders. In this next segment, I want us to focus on them and explain why they remain at the top since the days of Winston Churchill and go as far back as the days of Charles Darwin.

As we focus on these traits, we need to put them within the broader context of the theme – *From Alpha to Zen*. What role does character play in the direction of a thoughtful, inclusive, and considerate leader? What role does it play in the leadership of an authoritarian Alpha demagogue?

Predictability

Predictability is the consistency in character one displays, regardless of circumstances. It is also to be viewed as the expected response – based on past *behavior* – one brings to bear on a situation. In the realm of leadership, the world has witnessed predictability in both negative and positive ways. In Adolf Hitler, for example, the world expected nothing but unceasing trouble. He was predictably a man who schemed horror, led through hate-filled rhetoric, and presided over the planting of xenophobic tendencies. That kind of negative predictability has been associated with Alpha leadership.

Pol Pot and Amin Dada were similarly predictable in their erratic ways. They were men known to act in ways whose outcome was defined by mayhem and death. In recent days, America has given the world another predictable leader in Donald Trump. His predictability has led to worsening race relations, a disastrous response to a pandemic, and a collapse in the stock market. Many will admit that they knew what they were getting when they elected him. Many would agree that as human beings, we are all, in some ways, flawed. Perhaps, they hadn't considered how incredibly skilled Donald Trump was going to be at the game of power dynamics – or the way power affects a relationship between two or more people – and the potential negative impact of this on society.

On the other hand, positive predictability is what makes leaders great. The world has witnessed the predictability of Barack Obama, who went out of his way always to seek compromise and lead the world in forging a unity of purpose. We have also been witnesses to the Issa Brothers' predictability. These British moguls have acted only to grow their business and expand British products' reach globally. One is not to forget the predictability of the late tech mogul, Steve Jobs, whose core drive was to give the world newer ways of accessing information.

Yet, it isn't sufficient to see leaders as predictable or unpredictable or positive or negative. We need to understand that it is, in essence, *a choice* since each of us can demonstrate the positive and the negative forms of predictability.

Essentially thus, we say that an intrinsic behavior is linked to a core psychological preference.

Preference plays a crucial role in understanding how a leader might predictably behave. Consider rational choice theory, for example, the school of thought which proposes that individuals will use rational calculations to make rational choices and achieve outcomes that suit their self-interests and objectives. This cuts both ways – whether one will emerge an Alpha or a Zen leader. The difference is how one will process those choices and apply them for the greater good of society.

Consider the moral identity theory, the extent to which being a righteous person is important to a person's core identity and speaks to how we all integrate moral ideals in developing our characters. The degree to which being a moral person is important to a person's identity eventually sets them apart as either dependably Alpha in approach to life or Zen; participative or authoritarian.

The common denominator among the Zen leaders of the twentieth and the twenty-first century is that they had predictably positive character. The Alpha leaders had predictably negative character. Where a Zen leader united the world or the workers for a common purpose, an Alpha leader generated an atmosphere where tension, individualism, and fear became the order of the day.

Courageousness

Courageousness is the ability to remain sober, firm, and focused when under fire. It demonstrates a willingness to make unpopular decisions when a leader is certain; it is for the growth of an organization or nation or whatever institution is involved. When a leader acts with courage, the people they lead can generally empathize and work to help the leader succeed.

In the days leading up to the Falklands War, on 2 April 1982 – 14 June 1982, between the UK and Argentina, I can only imagine what went on through Prime Minister Margaret Thatcher's mind. She was aware of the cost of the war on human life. She had to have contemplated horrendous images that were likely to be splashed across the screens as television networks transmitted the element of human suffering, British losses, and as the British Pound and markets reacted to the news from the battlefield. Was the Prime Minister filled with fear? Did she face a moment of dread?

Courage is that rare ability to face potential danger front-on, evaluate a set of patently unfavorable options, and go with the one you believe to be least damaging. Margaret Thatcher weighed the cost of not attacking and concluded that inaction would be more costly in the long run than action. Therefore, a leader must be ready and willing to make a tough decision and be prepared to bear the palatable or grim *consequences*. It is based on the outcome of those tough decisions that leaders are later judged.

There are several factors we need to look into as we evaluate the overall performance of a leader against this quality:

a. Accountability. The saying goes – *the buck stops with the leader*. Accountability is the act of being held responsible for the decision/s one has made. In the political arena, it comes down during each election. It comes down when the board and voting stakeholders review the CEO's performance in the corporate world. A great leader is usually aware of their accountability to stakeholders and acts with them in mind.

b. Loneliness. Another saying goes – *it is rather lonely at the top*. Indeed, it is. It is, even when things go right. When they go wrong, the leader is left to carry the cross alone. Even those who voted to move the company in a given direction *disown* their vote. And when the time comes to hold the beleaguered leader to account, loneliness is ratcheted up by what feels like an act of sabotage and then betrayal. A great leader must have the fortitude of character to withstand the critical moments of setbacks that inevitably come to even the best leaders.

c. Global changes. A great leader must keep in tune with the rapid changes sweeping the globe and the impact on the venture they lead. In geopolitics, not too long ago, the world was embroiled in a cold war driven by the twin ideologies of market economics and socialism. World businesses were organized around that premise. Today, the world faces the prospect of a rising and fairly aggressive China. Brexit has brought into the mix a new element in Europe. The forces against globalization are active in the goal to whip up nationalistic sentiment in much of the Western world. These *powerful* forces can speedily transform the business landscape and cause dynamics that, if not managed well, may well sink a venture.

d. Stoicism. A seasoned leader must avoid the trap of bitterness and remain stoic. The so-called betrayals and undercutting are a normal part of what is to be expected in the field. Being a CEO or a president, or an admiral is not the end of life and must not be regarded as a do-or-die existence. Remain stoic. Leadership is being aware of how to interact with each situation positively. Courage is to remain composed when the battle has become overwhelming and win without leaving behind a wasteland of broken individuals or a collapsed vision.

Firmness

The other word for being firm is being emphatic. It is the act of being resolute, unyielding, or *dogged* about an issue or a direction one wants to go in. It is a *fine line* between stubbornness or recalcitrance on the one hand and benevolent dictatorship on the other. The kind of firmness I refer to in this segment is borne out of reason and contemplation rather than emotion.

For example, in the United States of America, we were all treated to a spectacle as President Donald Trump had rejected science as an approach to containing the spread of the Covid-19 virus. The Republican had remained firm in his belief that the virus is not a threat and that his base of far-right zealots would be charged enough to help reelect him – and this at a time, poll numbers point to fatigue with his zero-sum style of Alpha leadership. That boneheaded firmness is not what I am talking about.

Being emphatic is an art. There are several critical factors one must consider before adopting the strategy of firmness in dealing with a matter:

   a. Data. Let us refer to this as factual decision-making. A seasoned leader will act *only* after exhaustive data has allowed them to move in a particular direction. The decision they make will be anchored upon a foundation of evidence and studies backed by the credibility of the study's men and women. Where such a study has been conducted, a leader must be committed to the implementation and be willing to swim against the tide until such a time as all the others can see what they did not see earlier. I call it commonsense toughness.

Credibility of personnel. In the USA, Donald Trump had had excellent advice on the virus through virologist Dr. Anthony Fauci. He rejected the advice. A great leader must have the ability to assess his personnel's capabilities and trust their word once they are deployed. The key is to hire men and women with proven skills and knowledge to drive an agenda *forward*. Once again, leadership calls for toughness when a decision has been reached based on sound science, data, or intelligence only the leader has.

b. Resources. It is not wise to drive a matter when needed resources are not available to implement it. Toughness makes sense when all the elements required to get a matter off the ground successfully are in place. It is only at such a time that a leader can and must be tough in insisting that the time to go forward has come – otherwise, nothing will move.

Dependability

We have already talked about predictability. You are probably wondering what the difference is between *predictability* and *dependability*. Predictability – as we have already established –

has everything to do with guesswork. It involves estimating what actions one will take based on patterns of the past. On the other hand, dependability speaks to our being *worthy* or having earned another person's trust or confidence. One is dependable because they have acted a certain way through a long period of time and has thus established a character pattern.

The example of US President Donald Trump will suffice here again. Is he predictable in his ways? He has become predictably divisive on race and has shown repeated willingness to break with any number of commonsensical approaches. So, is he a man one may regard as dependable? Not at all. Such an individual cannot be reliable, for he is predictably unpredictable and therefore not worthy of anyone's confidence or trust.

Dependability calls for a certain number of core traits in one:

a. A good listener. A leader gradually evolves into a dependable character because of the rare ability to be a good listener. There is an element of dependability that runs through empathy and the willingness to walk in the shoes of someone else as you lead them out of whatever predicament is ongoing. Outstanding leadership is founded on the ability to set aside a minute to listen carefully and hear what a person is saying with the sole aim of solving a problem, not merely for the sake of it.

b. Honesty. For a great leader, his or her word is a bond. Honesty is a crucial aspect of being dependable because it is the only basis for people to take one's word seriously. Theresa May was intensely focused on her goal to exit Britain from the EU, but her honesty in how she was going about it was called into question – did she want Britain out or out but with a deal that kept her partially in? In the end, the public felt she was not to be trusted and replaced her with the bombastic Boris Johnson, who called it straight and thereby earned the trust of Britons. Boris became viewed as a more honest broker.

c. Proportionality. Those who have become great leaders have known to be proportional in their approaches, promises, and utterances. They have become aware that promises made are a debt owed. Such men and women have, therefore, known the value of being proportional. They make only promises they will fulfill. They utter only words they believe will be achievable. They engage only in approaches that will prove doable. In the end, they know that trust is earned and that to be dependable, one must *continually* be in a state of earning that trust.

d. Values. In a sense, a great leader becomes a brand *ambassador* or a reflection of people's core values. They become one to be regarded as dependable only because they are judged based on the ability to scrupulously adhere to the community's values. Donald Trump has failed this critical test because he has departed from the values America holds dear. In Israel, Benjamin Netanyahu has been dependable because he has been a reliable ambassador of the values of the Israelis. Core values, thus, are an essential aspect of dependable leadership.

We have dwelt on the matter of character because it is foundational to leadership. Through the key examples we have looked at, you get the sense that without being of a solid character – which lends itself to predictability, courage, dependability, and toughness, leadership becomes a *debilitating* burden; too heavy to bear.

Before I conclude this chapter with a moving story of Nelson Mandela, let me point out a positive consistency in thoughtful leaders' character is what earns them the description of a Zen leader. The negativity evidenced in the character of a cold, authoritative leader earns them the tag of an Alpha leader—character matters. Even at an early age, it points to the kind of individual one will become in life. Take this story, for example:

Nelson Mandela tells the story of the evening he went into a Pretoria restaurant to have tea. While at the restaurant, he sat across from one of the men who was a prison guard while he was locked up. The man was shocked to see him and started trembling. He was now the president of a free South Africa.

President Mandela asked the security men around him to order a cup of tea for the trembling man. It was only later when the guards asked Mandela why the man had been so afraid that he told them how that guard used to urinate on his head when he asked for water. "It was so humiliating!"

The president explained that in a new South Africa, the nation had turned a corner. The nation had a new character. But the incident said more about Mandela than the nation – that he was a dependable leader. The ideals he had espoused as a fighter for equality and justice were deeply locked in his heart and came out effortlessly even when he met those who had done him harm. Character is at the core of what great leadership is. It is who one truly is away from the prying eye of the public. It is the honest answer one gives to themselves when they ask – *who am I?*

In the next chapter, we take on another pivotal matter in leadership. Communication has been and remains regarded as the stabilizing hinge upon which the door of a venture turns. In the chapter ahead, our goal is to find an answer to the critical question – *what does effective communication look like?* How has effective communication transformed the leadership landscape of the twenty-first century?

CHAPTER 4

COMMUNICATION

Communication is regarded as the stabilizing hinge upon which the door of a venture turns. When we encounter the term communication, what jumps to mind is oratorical skills or the ability to wow an audience with flair. It is lost on us the fact that effective communication comes with several forms and styles that may suit one given occasion and not another. The leader's role is to understand the target audience and a communication method that will best deliver the message intended.

Here in the UK, one of the most successful TV programs was that of comedian Rowan Atkinson, who masterfully played Mr. Bean. Relying almost solely on mimicry and gestures, he perfected the rare art of communicating powerful, topical, and relevant messages to the audience. He became a hit not because he spoke the loudest or ever got truly animated, but because he communicated *effectively*, and people identified with the message.

In this chapter, our goal is to delve deeply into communication and understand why all the leaders who have gone on to excel have been adept at communicating their message. Whether it was Adolf Hitler in Germany, Richard Branson in the UK, Mother Teresa in India, Nelson Mandela in South Africa, or Donald Trump in the USA, how they communicated their vision defined their leadership style.

Having lumped leaders together – those we have vilified as despotic and dangerous and those we have praised as noble and exemplary – we are now compelled to define the term, communication. Why does it work for the villains and the nobles alike? What is it about communication that sets apart the great from the mediocre leaders? Why does it serve the Alpha and the Zen leader in equal measure?

Defining Communication

In the dictionary and other platforms, you have undoubtedly come across varying definitions of the term. As in many other matters, though, I want us to get to a derived meaning. The first place to go is to ask ourselves what kinds of approaches are available to one who wishes to communicate.

a.   Oratory. Not all leaders are gifted with this skill, but those who have it have succeeded where others have failed. In the USA, Barack Obama used his oratory to effectively communicate his core message and draw millions of people to the inspiring vision he had for the United States of America. For one to emerge an effective speaker, these elements are core:

- Reliance on facts.
- A receptive audience.
- Relevance of message.
- Speech as a rallying cry.

In Germany, Adolf Hitler deployed this very skill to devastating effect. He rallied the nation against the Jews and dramatically expanded the empire, using his *overwhelming* oratorical prowess to push an agenda that would eventually draw the ire of global powers unnerved by his expansionist drive. Oratory, therefore, remains one of the most effective ways to communicate.

b. Codes. Codes or suggestive language have been used by skillful leaders to effectively communicate elements of their messages that they do not wish to be expressed in layman's terms. While well-meaning leaders have applied this skill to advance a worthwhile cause, it has also been deployed by divisive leaders to cause upheavals. Hitler used codes to denigrate the Jews by calling attention to their physical features. Trump has cynically used codes to speak to white supremacists by giving a shout-out to a so-called silent majority. Communicating by way of codes almost always carries with it the element of us versus them – the notion that "this is for us, not for them." A great leader must understand how to use codes in a way that *uplifts* relationships and advances a cause rather than harms it.

c. Songs, poems, and lyrics. Leaders gifted in vocals may stray into singing or reading poetry or lyrics to communicate an aspect of their message. On the day sad Barack Obama showed up to eulogize a pastor who had been killed in Alabama, he gave a stirring speech on race relations, but when he eventually broke into the song Amazing Grace, the audience immediately rose up, and the atmosphere became electric. Jacob Zuma, the disgraced former president of South Africa, when he was given a moment to pay tribute to Nelson Mandela at the freedom fighter's funeral, did not say a word; he got behind the podium and broke into a powerful Zulu rendition. It so moved the audience that for the first time, tears flowed freely as people reflected on the words of the song. Leaders with the ability to use this communication skill have spoken straight to the heart.

Effective communication – it is essential to keep in mind that this only happens when a number of factors are in harmony with the message being put across. Thus, it is important to be aware of the message and what we would like our audience to take away; how we would like them to feel or act as a result of our communication. For example, you may be aware of the term, Neuro-Linguistic Programming (NLP). NLP is used by many successful individuals and relates to how we organize our thoughts, feelings, language, and behavior patterns.

NLP provides a methodology that we can use to *model* outstanding performance in communication. To be a successful NLP practitioner, we first need to understand how human beings create their unique internal map of the world in how we perceive, filter, and eventually distort information. People well-practiced in the modes of NLP understand how they can use techniques to modify their behavior in such a way as to improve confidence, self-awareness, and social interaction. NLP proposes that our views of the world affect how we exist and operate in the world and that it is necessary to move beyond those thoughts and behaviors that do not aid us and have not proven beneficial to us achieving our objectives.

The other matter of critical importance is how we perceive seasons and times. One might think this is a commonsense matter, but you will be stunned how many people have spoken out of turn just because they were not in tune with the season or the times. An effective communicator must be well informed and able to match his message with the times and prevailing circumstances.

Take the example of President Trump drumming up support for his reelection by referring to suburban women as *housewives*. This term was used in the 1950s to refer to white women in the suburbs, a racist reference that has no place in modern-day America. Donald Trump claimed that he had saved them from low-income housing programs that would invade their neighborhoods. Then there are the unfortunate words Oprah Winfrey uttered on her show when mad cow disease had ravaged England and was projected to hit the US soon. In April 1996, Howard Lyman, a former cattle rancher turned advocate for the vegan way of life, appeared on Oprah Winfrey's show. In response to his criticism of the practice of feeding processed livestock to cattle, which had been linked to the outbreak of mad cow disease in the UK, Oprah responded that his remarks "just stopped me cold from eating another burger." Her words caused a tremor within the industry as Americans shunned beef, and farmers felt the heat of falling profits and a sudden oversupply. She was sued in an Amarillo court and faced several days of trial in the Texas panhandle. The upshot of this is that it matters what season words are uttered in. What felt perfectly of good cheer in the fifties might not be wise to speak in the nineties. What was cool to say in the twentieth century may have no place in the twenty-first. We have to be aware of the seasons and the rules they come with to avoid speaking out of turn.

With that preamble, we are now at the point where we can define communication. Communication is the art of effectively conveying a message in a manner that causes the intended receiver to act or be moved to consider the message's impact. That is what effective communication means – it leads to action. If what you are saying falls on deaf ears, either you have failed to communicate, or whatever you are communicating is out of season.

Articulation of Vision

In an earlier chapter, we characterized vision as the most important element in leadership. Indeed, it is. How it is articulated, therefore, is foundational to how a venture will evolve. Leadership comes down to how the beholder of a vision can paint a clear picture of where they seek to guide the venture. Jeff Bezos and Jack Ma, and Bill Gates had to have found a way to enthrall workers with the powerful visions they had dreamt up for an interconnected world. That Microsoft and Amazon, and Alibaba have evolved into the world's most profitable trendsetters in business is a testament to the fact that these leaders succeeded in conveying their visions from their heads to the heads of their workers. They communicated their imagery of the world in a manner others could paint it.

To articulate a powerful vision, a leader needs to communicate it a certain way:

a. Passionately. To watch Jack Ma or Mandela or Civil Rights leader Martin Luther King Jr. speak is to watch a speech delivered with passion. The sense that what is being conveyed is heartfelt is left in no doubt. It is as if the communicator is saying *we must do this, or we'll perish; our very lives depend on it.* Passion may manifest in a cracking voice, forming tears or mannerisms like a shaking hand or rapidly blinking eyes. When those being addressed see passion on display, the tendency is to give the matter thought and eventually act on it.

b. Repetitively. An important matter will not be spoken about once and forgotten; it will be repeated time and again so that it settles in the mind of those needed to act on it. At the height of the campaign for Brexit, it was on display how Boris Johnson talked about the many benefits of delinking from Europe at every stop. He repeated the same message until much of Britain agreed with him and gave him a chance to turn his core thoughts into action for the country. Great communicators have always understood the value of repetitiveness in driving a message.

c. Urgency. If it is to be *regarded* as important, it has to be urgent. In Martin Luther King Junior's *I Have a Dream Speech*, he shared that, "It would be fatal for the nation to overlook the urgency of the moment." In Mahatma Gandhi's *Quit India* message of 1942, he shared, "As I view the situation, they are on the brink of an abyss. It, therefore, becomes my duty to warn them of their danger even though it may, for the time being, anger them to the point of cutting off the friendly hand that is stretched out to help them." Such carefully crafted messages are designed to whip up a sense of urgency and create an atmosphere where action is prioritized.

The first and the most significant role of communication in a venture is to paint the vision in such clear terms that those meant to act on it do so. Where communication fails to articulate a vision properly, there is a good chance the venture will go on to fail.

Speaking with Authority

At a time Britain had become the sick man of the world due to Prime Minister Theresa May's stunning inability to find the formula for a working partnership with the EU, Boris Johnson stepped in and spoke with unflinching authority about his vision and how he was going to accomplish it. One may have disagreed with him, but he certainly seemed like he had a coherent plan. The authority with which he spoke was refreshing after months of a stalemate in Brussels, in Parliament, and within the political parties in the land.

I do not know of any world leader who has failed to project authority and went on to be great. Yet to speak with authority does not necessarily mean flair in speech; it means reliance on:

a. Facts. Facts may also be viewed as data or findings. People are keen on facts because they give the needed assurance of a derived solution to a matter. People often want to understand the what, why, how, where, and when. *It didn't just happen, or it wasn't reached on a whim.* Corporate leaders like Jack Ma and Aliko Dangote have relied on research to settle on paths that have led to successes beyond their wildest dreams. A leader who relies on facts wins confidence.

b. Perspective. The real mystery of leadership resides in perspective. When a leader gets up to speak, their listeners want to learn something new or see something from a different perspective that might change or reinforce their opinion on a subject. It is of no use to stand behind a podium and regurgitate the same stuff already in the public domain. The reason the world tuned in to listen to Bill and Melinda Gates – at the height of the killer Covid-19 pandemic – was because they knew things the rest of us did not know. As the founders of the Bill and Melinda Gates Foundation, they were updated on all the dangerous pandemic aspects. They had pertinent information on the development and research into an approvable vaccine. The power of perspective, therefore, cannot be overstated.

c. Associations. Have you ever wondered why the Prime Minister appears with the health secretary when reporting on Covid-19 or *any* aspect of health? Have you wondered why the Prime Minister is usually flanked by the military chief when giving updates on Syria or Iran or any global hotspot? It is because such professional associations confer credibility on the message they are delivering. No leader is all-knowing, and people know that; it, therefore, helps to be covered by professionals whose advice is believed to have formed the basis of the message being communicated. That is how authority is earned on any matter.

Harmonizing Thought, Direction, and Action

In closing this chapter, it bears pointing out that all the factors we have handled must find harmony in the communicator for effectiveness to be achieved. A communicator who lacks empathy, does not inspire confidence through certainty, or does not speak with authority, will fail to communicate.

Clarity of a message is only achieved when a communicator deploys all the elements we have discussed in this chapter at any given time. It is through communication that a leader can guide the ship of a venture toward a given port. The lack of effective communication will also run the same ship into an iceberg of disillusionment, grumbles, and discontent.

Having dealt with the crucial matter of communication, it is time to turn our attention to an equally important issue. In the twenty-first century, we have observed that changes occur at a breakneck speed. What we once regarded as settled matters are challenged and discarded as new facts emerge and confounding discoveries open *frontiers* we never knew existed. A modern leader is left with no choice but to remain on the cutting edge of trends and emerging dynamics in leadership.

The question we seek to answer in the new chapter is: Is it possible for a modern leader to continually remain on the cutting edge of trends globally and how they impact leadership? Can a delusional, self-praising Alpha leader be open to trends and changes transforming global commerce and setting trailblazing dynamics in international relations? How about a pragmatic Zen leader?

This is the one area in which you are about to find out that the Alpha leader falters because of ego, the imagination that they know it all. On the other hand, the Zen leader senses the need to surrender to dictates of changes and applies them to his or her advantage. Lest I say more than I need to, let me end it there and invite us to the next chapter – **The Cutting-Edge Leader.**

CHAPTER 5

THE CUTTING-EDGE LEADER

In the twenty-first century environment, we have come to the point where getting rusty can be swift and brutal. A leader worth his or her salt has to be alert and immersed in global trends that will affect business by changing the nature of the external and internal environments, usher in new competitors, and introduce the element of a shrinking market share for hitherto monopolistic products.

It is not enough that a leader paints the scope of a vision; they have to retain a healthy ability to be at the forefront of reading market trends well and acting in time to stave off potentially ruinous acts or factors that may sink the company. Being a reactionary leader does not cut it in this bold, new century; what the world needs is proactive leaders who spot dangers and opportunities ahead of time and positions their companies to act.

It is incredible how the world has become so intricately interconnected that whatever affects the Unites States or Britain or Australia, or the Middle East can cause turbulence in world markets. China has evolved into a superpower with the ability to destabilize or cause needed market stability in the southeastern realm of the world. Saudi Arabia and several Middle Eastern nations have steadily evolved into powerful OPEC nation-members with the enviable ability to determine world oil prices and the power to bulldoze their way because of the precious commodity.

What may be lost on many of us is the impact of the world's oil supply on general trade and service-delivery worldwide. The shop owner on the street in Chicago will be affected by either a shortage that leaders of oil price hikes or a slug that will lead to low demand. Whatever affects *transport* in the world inevitably alters the programs and routes and general outlook in shipping. This leads to an inevitable rethink in commodity pricing and the speed with which services are delivered.

In the realm of political leadership, especially in the nations that bear the brunt of decisions with the ability to shake markets, being well informed is not an option. A leader of any of the G-8 countries, and most of the global, regional heavyweights, must be aware of the goings-on around the world to act in time should such a need suddenly arise. Despite what anti-globalization voices and shrill nationalist proponents claim, the world has receded into a global village, where an apocalyptic environmental disaster in Europe can shut down crucial transport networks and lead to a global chain reaction of key losses and an unforeseen market shrinkage.

A conflagration between Israel and any major oil supplier in the Middle East – especially if it leads to a blockade of the Suez Canal – can harm global oil supply and similarly harm world business.

The net impact of global interconnectedness in commerce is that a leader has to be aware of what is happening in every part of the world because it will inevitably have a cascading effect that may well find its way to their shores.

Defining a Cutting-Edge Leader

A cutting-edge leader is one who has made the *wise* decision to fastidiously remain connected to global trends to make informed decisions that impact business and people's lives. The question to ask here, therefore, is, what traits define a leader with a knack for top-of-the-range acumen?

a. Restlessness. This term is deployed here in a most positive sense. A restless leader is a man or woman whose sole motivation is to drive a company toward success. Such a leader wakes up each day to focus solely on *strategies* that will propel the company toward maximum productivity, increased market share, and a corporate culture geared toward and aligned with the overall vision. It is toward a winning brand that a restless leader becomes focused and may, at times, seem even "strange."

b. Results-oriented. A results-oriented leader is keen on setting goals and ensuring they are achieved. They are oriented toward setting dates, deadlines, deliverables, and other ways of tracking performance so that expected results are achieved. Not too long ago, the world lost one of the most results-oriented leaders in the business community when the Samsung CEO died. From a small and unheard-of brand, Lee transformed the company into a global leader in electronics by doggedly going for results. He *succeeded* beyond his wildest expectations.

c. Happy warrior. To be a happy warrior is to enjoy what one is doing. A leader who loves what they are doing will inevitably get outside the comfort zone and seek new ways of making things work faster and a lot more efficiently. You see major changes in football clubs all over Europe because the managers are happy warriors. They feel inclined to go after that great striker, that great goalkeeper, that successful midfielder. The idea is to add one element that will propel the team to the top and win the league. Naturally, a leader in the field of football will seek to understand trends and be aware of breaking stories if only to scheme ways to upstage others.

d. Smartness. One who seeks to be a great leader must become smart first. There are two types of *smartness*, though:

- Book smart. This is as a result of extensive academic orientation. A book smart leader will tend to be great with theory and verbosity but may not prove successful where it concerns profit margins.

- Street smart. This results from delving deep into the terrain and understanding the dynamics that make a system move.

Smartness is key to relevant leadership in the twenty-first century. The world is not as kind to inept leadership as it once was. Any leader, as soon as they are introduced, is instantly judged based on knowledge. A leader who displays a vast command of issues and can competently articulate them becomes regarded as a modern leader.

e. Empathetic. This is critical. All great leaders express the quality of humanness in leading human beings. It is vital to learn how to lead people, to empathize with them so that all decisions made consider their core interests and feelings. In this age of artificial intelligence (AI), when many leaders are predisposing the world toward machines in production, it has never been more critical for leaders to put themselves in the shoes of their workers. The need to understand the fears, joys, and expectations of workers has never been more urgent. Empathy is what drives a cutting-edge leader to do what they must to understand subjects or workers or citizens.

That is clearly another long, derived definition of a cutting-edge leader. What we now want to answer is the question of how. How does one remain on top of emerging trends in leadership in the twenty-first century? This is a critical matter because the grim danger of incremental rustiness and eventual irrelevance becomes acuter with time, leading to a situation where morale dissipates, productivity drops, and a general malaise takes hold.

Due to the important nature of this subject matter, we need to look at the element of tools or aides that make a leader a cutting edge one with the focus it deserves. Harry S. Truman, the 33rd president of the USA, famously said, "Not all readers become leaders, but all leaders must be readers." Let us start with books:

Books

This may sound obvious, but books and related publications are an excellent tool for remaining on the cutting edge of leadership trends. The subject of leadership has lately been treated with such *urgency* that schools, departments, and libraries have been built purely to address this matter. What you find in such facilities are books written by some of the top leadership practitioners in the world. It is also true time has changed the way we access books – for those who appreciate different modes. Some people now prefer the spoken word, so there has been a trend toward having authors narrate their books or dramatize them. Blinkist's professional book summary service offers key insights from over 3,000 bestselling non-fiction books in 15 minutes or less. Leaders can boost their knowledge and discover new perspectives on subjects of interest. With Audible, the world's largest selection of audiobooks and original podcasts can be enjoyed "anytime, anywhere" via their app.

It is our lucky break that men like Nelson Mandela and Tony Blair; and women like Oprah Winfrey and Professor Wangari Mathai, the Nobel-winning environmentalist in Kenya, have written books to speak to their experiences as leaders. Those are books a modern leader must read.

More relevant, though, are books written in the recent past by leaders engaged in the trade at the time – Elon Musk, Jack Ma, Hillary Clinton, and Christiane Amanpour of CNN.

In their various fields, these leaders have gone through unique experiences and can speak to the changing nature of the political, social, and economic environment in the world. They have delved into the impact of such changes in leaders and in those they lead. Picking their brains on critical leadership trends through their books is a worthy and urgent endeavor for any leader today.

Naturally, not all leaders are wired the same. There are those who want to read the same information from different genres of books:

a. Textbook. Not surprisingly, most leaders fall into the category of readers who seek to gain knowledge by reading a textbook. They view the textbook as an authentic manner to interact with serious subjects. Indeed, the textbook approaches its subject matter in a matter-of-fact way and gets to its point in a laborious, researched, and scholarly manner that lends credence to claims of its firmness in the delivery of information.

b. Novel. Novelist John Grisham, with his legal thrillers, Robin Cook, with his medical thrillers, and Dan Brown, with his mystery thrillers, have perfected the art of discussing elements in their trade with gusto. In the realm of leadership, the world is beginning to see clear efforts at the leadership novel, but they are not as well developed as those in other fields. Going by the interest novels in different fields has generated, it is possible that when known authors release the leadership novels, they will be another great tool in a cutting-edge leader's arsenal.

c. Fables. By far, this has emerged as the most popular leadership genre out in the market. Leadership gurus like Robin Sharma and Robert Kiyosaki have weaved personal and fictional stories into tales that have wowed their readers and inspired them to become better people and better leaders. Digging into modern concepts – credit cards, bank loans, research, startups – they have created a sense that what one needs in abundance are focus, inspiration, and resilience to succeed in the twenty-first century.

Books tend to be expensive, and the time to read them may be limited due to the squeezed nature of the time we have at our disposal. However, it is crucial to read voraciously to remain relevant in the brutally unforgiving realm of modern leadership. A modern leader is only as relevant as they are in tune with trends that expand, broaden, and cause a company to grow from strength to strength.

Magazines and Journals

We are referring to magazines and journals aligned with leadership or a relevant area of professional growth. The Harvard School of Business has one of the most authoritative journals that address trends and leadership themes. It has become a popular and relaxing way for leaders to acquaint themselves with socio-economic and political acts shaping the marketplace in today's world.

Remaining on the cutting edge also demands that leaders become aware of occurrences outside their areas of interest. For example, it does not hurt to be mindful of what goes on in Hollywood through *People* and other glitzy magazines of that nature. It doesn't hurt to be aware of the goings-on in Israel, Armenia, South Africa, or Austria by reading *The Economist*. It does not hurt to immerse in political and business trends in the USA by reading *Time* or *Forbes* magazine.

Beefed up with colorful images and *relatable* stories, magazines have become an essential medium for telling humanity's powerful stories. Smart Leaders have viewed them as a critical way to keep a finger on the pulse of those they lead – because man is changing just as rapidly as the forces shaping the world today are changing. The ignorant, powerless worker of yesterday has been replaced by the twenty-first century's bold, unionized worker. Any leader eager to understand the changed nature of the worker or citizen today does well to read the magazines and journals that speak to these issues.

Naturally, limited with time, a leader will find it not so easy to read all the magazines under the sun, but there are key ones a great leader must make a must-read:

a. *The Economist* deals with issues worldwide and is regarded as the world's most authoritative magazine today.

b. *Time* magazine remains an authoritative take on political, social, and economic trends in the USA. Because America remains a global superpower, it is important to be keyed on occurrences in Congress, Senate, Supreme Court, the White House, and even in the state capitals.

c. *Forbes* magazine. This magazine is a crucial tool in a leader's arsenal because of its refreshing nature of tracking business trends worldwide. With sister publications like *Forbes Africa* and *Forbes Asia*, it is a leader in setting trends and alerting business leaders to changes taking place that may *immediately* or at a later date impact their work.

d. *Health Digest.* Due to the nature of leadership today, leaders are always on the move. Traveling overseas has become a key feature for many. With it has come dangerous health conditions like clots and hypertension, and dietary complications. Health magazines are a great way to keep up to date with the latest thinking about those health factors that can help keep a leader in good form, maintaining good brain function, sustained energy, and physical resilience.

Magazines and journals are essentially cheaper than books and are easier to manage. A leader eager to see his workers grow in skill and wisdom may want to consider subscribing to the key magazines related to the nature of business they handle. It does not hurt anything to add to the mix *entertainment* magazines that are purely for relaxation.

Television

We need not dwell too much on this. Let it suffice to say that the world is now at a point where television networks serve key regions with roots and a keen interest in their specific geography. In the Arab world, Al Jazeera has emerged as a pivotal network. In the West, CNN, BBC, and France 24 have emerged as the leading disseminators.

Due to the influx of networks with a global reach, a leader today is served by professionals able to help them digest global affairs and tie events in one part of the world to business prospects in his or her neck of the woods.

In recent days – due to this realization – most companies have moved in the direction of placing a screen at a strategic location where workers can watch newscasts, documentaries, and programs that acquaint them with current events.

Suppose a leader is not a TV enthusiast and won't find time to watch sports or programs on space or sea exploration. In that case, they should at least watch news and current affairs programs to be aware of threats that may snowball into mushrooming clouds with the ability to affect local business eventually. It is a dereliction of duty not to be adequately informed.

Newspapers and Online News

You will notice that most newspapers are designed in a remarkably similar manner — with a segment for politics, business, technology, science, travel, entertainment, and sports. Due to this consistent nature, newspapers carry information that is up-to-date and usable immediately.

While the magazines, journals, and books may provide information with a broad scope, newspapers gravitate toward current events and reflect the now. A leader can make core decisions based on reports drawn from the pages of a newspaper. Thus, if costs prohibit any leader from availing the *Harvard Business Review* in his or her lobby, they should be sure to make provision of newspapers for employees and all cadres of leaders in the company.

It is notable, though, that newspapers, much like other news outlets, have allied themselves with a given philosophy. *The New York Times* is primarily viewed as a left-leaning daily. *The Washington Post* is viewed in much the same manner. It is not a bad idea for newspapers to ally with a philosophy, but it is bad for a leader to fail to discern which philosophical tilt the paper leans toward.

At the end of the day, when it comes to advertising in a given paper, what counts is not the liberalness or conservatism of it, but the number of readers it reaches – to maximize product exposure. Indeed, the company's PR or advertising wings can quickly seek statistics and avail them as needed. A leader needs to have that total picture in mind for effectiveness in the decisions to be made.

Seminars and Workshops

Seminars and workshops are crucial to leadership in the twenty-first century. They bring together men and women who have proven themselves to be top in their fields. Not only are the moderators drawn from a pool of the absolute best, but so are the delegates sent in to learn from the gurus.

In a world where changes are a constant, it helps to attend as many seminars and workshops as one can – to learn new elements in the field and share successes experienced in the other places. Cutting edge leadership demands that we avail ourselves of *opportunities* that will make the ventures we run maximize output and play a leading role in expanding an economy.

Jack Ma has visited several countries to speak at workshops meant to spark economic growth by building leaders' capacity. Barack Obama – when he was President of the United States of America – visited Kenya with a long list of global business moguls to link up startups with established names in various trades. At the Gigiri Complex, he challenged top leaders in business to network with the developing ones for the sake of global economic expansion and the spreading of opportunity to all.

Travels

Richard Quest of CNN has excelled in bringing us programs on smart business traveling, a world of wonder, and incisive Wall Street trends. Whereas it is important to watch Quest to catch up on key business trends around the world, watching does not ever replace physical presence. It is on visits to places one has never been before that *new* elements are learned, and the mind is freed to *explore* certain possibilities that had never been considered.

An African leader will do well to visit Europe and the USA to learn how to positively handle competitive politics, free-market economics, and the elusive element of handing over power. In like manner, an American or European leader needs to visit Africa and areas of the world characterized as the third world to learn the impact of Washington and London's decisions on people they don't ever get to see but who are affected by their actions.

Traveling opens one's eyes and broadens his or her scope. It accords one an opportunity to evaluate where they stand in the measure of success as weighed on the global stage. It is even healthier when such travels are undertaken without the added pressures of work-related assignments and visits associated with family trauma – so that one is freed to slowly digest what they see.

In the end, any leader who remains confined to a local setting can only imagine and ascribe solutions with a local flavor. Such a leader will *lack* the ability to innovate and broaden the scope of solutions for fear of the unknown. Yet, in a world rapidly and continually going in a new direction with twists and turns, old solutions quickly run their course and are rendered useless. There is a need to ensure that a leader can borrow global best practices and boost a company's morale and productivity based on what has been learned.

Writing

This has not been an area many leaders are keen on, especially those outside the United States of America. However, leaders should do some research and writing so that their ideas are played alongside those of comparable leadership in their specialty. In the USA, just about every key leader has written a book, whether in politics, business, or religion. Professors are also in the race to write books and contribute articles to magazines where they seek to be read by peers.

Writing sharpens the mind. It makes one have to sit and reflect on issues. A leader who believes they have excelled in leadership needs to find time to share with the world, the skills, challenges, pains, and successes of their tenure. Jack Welch of the GE fame wrote a powerful memoir with his wife to share anecdotes of life as a successful American CEO. The book has been read by many who viewed him as a successful leader in business. Other notable leaders like Tony Blair, Jack Ma, Nelson Mandela, and Margaret Thatcher have also written about their experiences. But what's better than writing moving memoirs is writing about the journey while still in office.

It does not hurt to add the impressive title of author to the many accolades one carries as testimonials to a life lived to its fullest. Who knows, maybe by becoming an esteemed author, one may become a keynoter or consultant in addition to being a leader of a given company. Who does not want a dollar or pound or shilling extra if it can be made?

Cutting-edge leadership is what twenty-first-century leadership is about. It removes the burden of stress from an operation when a leader is well informed and is ready to experiment with bold, new ideas safely. On that note, we need to move on to the next key issue in leadership. Did you know that the quality of leadership one offers is directly tied to the degree to which one is willing to be innovative? Are you aware that Alpha leadership flounders because of lack of innovation and Zen leadership flourishes because of it?

In the next chapter, we want to discuss how being *innovative* will impact one's leadership. The concern we seek to address is the impact of innovation on the nature of *leadership* one can offer.

CHAPTER 6

THE INNOVATOR

As a little girl, I often watched as my father, after lunch, would collect the bones from the pork chops my mum had prepared and then go into his workshop, emerging sometime later with a pair of earrings or a brooch for my mother. On this little island of Grenada, my dad was considered a visionary, an innovator, and a pioneer. Not because he turned bones into brooches but because of his number of firsts. In 1959 just coming out of his twenties, he set up the first local insurance on the island, a company he named Western International. This company's formation enabled him to invite one of the world's largest companies to Grenada, Swiss Re-insurance. Today, Grenada can boast of numerous local and independent insurance companies because of this bold and ambitious initiative.

My dad represented a steamship that plied between Grenada and England. Of course, that ship had other ports of call in the West Indies. Quite often, when that ship arrived in Grenada from St. Vincent or Barbados, it would not have space for all the passengers booked from Grenada. Therefore, daddy would charter a plane from America to airlift these passengers, often more than one hundred people, and this would happen every two weeks. Thus, he launched the first charter flight agency in Grenada. He was the first to establish a company that supplied ready-mix concrete to the construction industry, importing trucks from overseas. I could go on. Suffice to say, that is where I learned my early lessons about innovation and innovative thinking.

This chapter, if you will, is the one that carries the weight of this book. Innovation is so critical to the survival of an entity we have to anchor *every* aspect of leadership on it. You will also discover that this is where Zen leadership profoundly diverges from Alpha leadership – the willingness to be creative.

In the previous chapters, I have mentioned the term innovation and even briefly referred to it as the successful implementation of creative ideas within a company or a nation to improve performance. In this chapter, we will dig deeper into the meaning and impact of innovation on a company's performance. Most startups, mid-level companies, and giant operations have become aware of innovation's centrality in driving performance and have gone all out to attract the most innovative employees. Because of this matter's deep and anchoring role, it is incumbent upon us to work with an expanded definition. So, what is innovation?

Innovation Defined

It is the successful implementation of creative ideas within a company to improve performance. It has been referred to as the exploration of new possibilities and the subsequent successful implementation of them. Thus, it is not about merely getting new ideas and the generation of an invention, but about the successful exploitation and diffusion of that very invention.

As one might imagine, innovation within a company is a multidimensional concept. It includes aspects like:

a. Product innovation, as in modifications to an existing design, core components, and product architecture.

b. Process or operations innovation is more about refining the methodologies in place to achieve far greater efficiency in the processes, leading to maximum output.

c. Technology innovation, which includes:

- Manufacturing technology.
- Information technology.

d. Management systems and organizational innovations, which advocate for concerns such as:

- Production control.
- Quality management.
- Changes in the company, such as decentralization of key authority and empowerment.

That is a long and packed definition of the term, innovation, but it will come in handy as we delve deeper into the matter. At the back of our minds, what we need to remember is that innovation is about finding creative ways to boost performance in a company at the end of the day. In the setting of a corporation, it gets more complicated because corporations exist to maximize output and deliver greater profits. Any corporation that fails to post profits, based solely on demonstrable and a corresponding rise in the indicators of rising performance, is to be viewed with jaundiced eyes, and its management may face undesirable measures as a result.

Approaches to Innovation

The first point to make here is that there are two distinct approaches to innovation:

- Exploration of new knowledge.
- Exploitation of existing knowledge.

Companies that explore new knowledge generally seek incremental scientific improvements to serve existing products or markets or break away from the safety of existing products or markets, to pursue bold new product ideas and create new markets. If this sounds drastic, it is. Therefore, the question is: what would cause a company to abandon the so-called safety of an existing product line to explore a new product and market?

a. Raw Product shortfalls. This occurs when the raw product the company has depended on for its production is depleted or is in danger of being classified, based on *new* evidence, as hazardous to human health and a threat to the environment.

b. Community hostility. This is a company's external environment factor – how it relates to the community in which it is established. This means that the company's management has failed to connect well with the host community, and community leaders have revolted against it, demanding it be moved. Deteriorations of this nature may cause a company to evaluate whether, by relocating to a new setting, it would still be profitable to carry on with the existing product and market or explore newer products.

c. Unfair competition. This occurs when a new player with superior product quality and a larger share of the market moves into the local market. It is a phenomenon that leaves the established company vulnerable and causes a reassessment of its viability in the face of detrimental competition.

d. Economic challenges. Companies are faced with unforeseen challenges whenever there is a sudden economic downturn. In the thirties' global depression, many companies had to either change products or markets or be shut down. I view it as a decision made in pain when a company's board must act to save it from permanent closure.

e. Political upheavals. In Africa and other politically unstable parts of the world, politics can significantly impact business operations. In nations like Uganda, Angola, and Burundi, companies have had to change products or even shut down because of instability and gross interference in business by corrupt state agents and political heavyweights.

As we discuss approaches to innovation, we need to mention that there are distinct variations of innovation. They are:

a. Incremental product innovation. These are generally lower-cost improvements, and small upgrades to existing concepts can be adopted relatively quickly. Improvements are often recommended by those engaged in the production process or by users of the product.

b. Radical innovation or breakthrough innovation. It may also be viewed as quantum leap innovation. It happens relatively fast, and its impact on the company is profound.

c. Organizational and technological or in-the-loop innovation. This is an innovation that focuses on matters of operations. In a sense, this is where a company is to rise or fall – it is key!

Incremental Product Innovation

Incremental innovation refers to applied science that searches for incremental improvements to existing know-how or adds value to the existing products for existing markets. This is the form of innovation that is common – much more common than the high-risk research type. It may seem like a lazy approach and may strike one as overly cautious. Still, companies prefer to look for low-risk ways to improve existing products' design, using current knowledge to serve today's markets.

Larger and much more established companies tend to be more risk-averse and prefer innovations that have a greater chance of making money, even if it means the potential returns will be less than spectacular. Such organizations typically have a large, installed customer base and a more geographically dispersed supply chain. For them, the central innovation challenge is to, at all times, move the performance bar a little higher without losing the ability to keep a complex set of technological and core business relationships arranged in an orderly manner. These companies are at a point where they prefer gradual, incremental innovations and tend to delay more fundamental innovations for as long as possible.

Breakthrough Innovation

Exploring new knowledge is well-illustrated by basic science and is often pursued in corporate research and development labs and university research centers. We have referred to breakthrough technology as a *quantum leap* because it enables a giant stride and engineers revolutionary changes in how a corporation is managed.

Organizational Innovation

It is also called management innovation. It involves exploring new business models, management techniques and strategies, and organizational structures. The attempt to create new products and services may spur organizational innovation, such as new business models arising to take advantage of newly-discovered opportunities.

One of the cardinal reasons for organizational innovation is that established companies can lose not just their ability to innovate but their insight into the necessity to innovate.

Complacency can set in as management gets comfortable with the way things are. Of course, the danger is that sooner, rather than later, the company loses its competitive advantage in product superiority and may lose its market share as a result.

The other way to state what I have just said is this – successful companies often become blind to opportunities other than those that sustain their current customer base. As companies sell *technologically* advanced and feature-rich products to serve the existing customers, they fail to sustain continuous innovations that would benefit new customers in new ways. The problem is complacency.

By achieving a higher mastery of technology and a higher mastery of product complexity, companies tend to risk losing a sense of how best to respond to customers whose requirements for simplicity override their need for the most technologically advanced products. Indeed, some are left behind when products become way too complicated for their comprehension. This is a critical phenomenon that does not affect industrialized nations only; it affects even those in the third world, as they move to emulate others.

In simpler terms, business process innovations are the efficient use of all key factors of a business to make them work in coordinated harmony to maximize output. What the Ford Motor Corp did in Detroit, Michigan, other companies have done as well. In Africa, innovators with an understanding of how systems interact to create an atmosphere conducive to efficiency have been in increasingly high demand. It is no wonder that several African corporations, like those run by Aliko Dangote and Strive Masiyiwa, are doing as well as corporations in the West.

Therefore, the question one might ask is – does a company do better with risk-taking executives, or is a company better off with cautious, risk-averse managers? The answer is in the nature of a given company. If a company is young and is in the early days of existence, it has far greater room to experiment with ideas. A company may also have room to innovate if it has been on a decline and needs to get back on track.

Risk-taking needs to be viewed as a *seasonal* matter, an activity to be engaged in by executives who have already taken care of the basics of ensuring the business's financial stability. I am not saying risk-taking will not pay off, but what if innovation backfires?

Bringing it Together

Inevitably, it had to come together. Through the years of metamorphosis in the definition of innovation, we have witnessed evidence that researchers and business leaders have remained attuned to relevant changes and trends. Five main areas have been identified as key when one innovates:

- Product innovativeness.

- Market innovativeness.

- Process innovativeness.

- Behavioral innovativeness.

- Strategic innovativeness.

It would be a neglect of duty if we failed to point out that certain studies signal the need for a critical balance between radical and incremental innovation. Though it is the case that radical or breakthrough innovations can harvest handsome financial profits, the largest percentage of most company revenue is still more likely to come from incremental innovation. Balancing core efforts to capture the advantages of both can be a wise but challenging goal for companies to pursue.

Let us conclude this chapter with two stories that best illustrate the power of innovation. Here is the first:

Combat Jet Mishaps

The US Air Force knew it had a problem in its hands on the fateful day it lost nineteen pilots as they carried out routine training maneuvers. There had been prior crashes, bungled landings, unintended dives, and obliteration of facilities as the supersonic aircraft landed. Not surprisingly, and in keeping with US military policy, multiple inquiries were launched to establish the cause of the mishaps and fatal accidents.

We are talking about the 1940s, the era of faster jets, jet-powered aviation, split-second decisions in the cockpit. Suppose nothing was done to establish the cause of the pilot's inability to control the planes. In that case, there were going to be more losses when the military was intent on developing even faster combat jets.

The conclusion reached by officials tasked to carry out the inquiries was startling. They blamed the growing mishaps on the fact that the cockpits were designed with the average 1926 man in mind. The dimensions applied to build the cockpit were dependent on years of military philosophy that worked with the concept of averages when handling core issues and designing sophisticated war machinery.

It would later take the skepticism of Lt. Gilbert S. Daniels to expose the flaw in this philosophy. The lieutenant was a rookie. He hadn't worked in the Air Force for long. He was troubled by the notion that the cockpit had been designed with an *average* pilot in 1926 in mind. In his Aero Medical Laboratory in Ohio, the lieutenant went to work to disabuse the military of the prevailing philosophy.

A physical anthropologist, he measured the thumb length, crotch height, and distance from a pilot's eyes to ears – a sample of 4,000 pilots. To the amazement of the lieutenant, there was no single pilot who had similar measurements as the next – they were all different. He concluded that they were nothing like averages. The military had relied on years of a faulty philosophy to run its critical affairs. It had led to mishaps and fatalities!

The philosophy of averages was further disproved when Dr. Robert L. Dickinson and a collaborator, Abram Belskie, sculpted the figure of an attractive woman based on size-data collected from 15,000 young adult women. In the end, Dr. Dickinson presented the sculpture, named Norma, as the ideal woman – in height, weight, and other attributes. It was a difficult act to follow for many women who, despite trying to match Norma, fell short by becoming obese, anorexic, and retaining stubborn fat in places they were powerless to change.

In 1952, Daniels wrote, "It is virtually impossible to find an average airman not because of any unique traits in this group but because of the great variability of bodily dimensions, which is characteristic of all men." Then instead of recommending that people be encouraged to work harder to conform to an arbitrary norm, he suggested that if the military wished to improve the soldiers' performance, it was the environment that had to change and conform to the individual – not the other way around. The air force then demanded that all cockpits were manufactured to fit pilots whose measurements fell within the five percent to ninety-five percent range on every dimension. Today, even the cockpits in our vehicles, seats, seatbelts, mirrors, headrests, and steering wheel are all adjustable to individual fit, as are our office chairs.

The Rise of Post-it

Spencer Silver was recruited as a chemist for 3M, a Minnesota multinational organization. In his years of work, he increasingly developed better adhesives for the company and was regarded as one of the most prolific adhesive engineers of his time. While researching to create bigger, stronger, tougher adhesives, he discovered something unusual: an adhesive that stuck only lightly to surfaces and didn't bond tightly to them. The microspheres' unique characteristics meant that the sticky substance could be peeled away without leaving residue and reused.

It would later take many years from the time the sticky yellow squares technology was developed to the time it eventually hit the market as a Post-it product. It all began when a colleague named Art Fry, who was aware of the reusable adhesive, approached Silver and suggested that they apply the adhesive to paper. Art also sang in the church choir and became frustrated with losing his hymn notes from his songbook. He thought he could use the sticky note to mark pages in his songbook since the loose papers he had been using were always falling out.

Silver did not object. One thing led to another. Their colleagues began to use the yellow squares to leave notes for one other. The importance of the squares started to reveal itself. Finally, when it had become evident that the invention was a worthy addition to communication, it would take a change in management before the company would take it up. They suddenly wanted to find out what the technology behind the yellow square was, eager to patent the innovation. 3M has since developed the innovation under the name, Post-it and produces fifty billion – of the once derided yellow squares – per year.

If you are beginning to wonder whether the issues we have covered in the earlier chapters are possible in every part of the world, you are right—location matters. The prevailing political, social-cultural and economic environment in which a company or a nation is *located* will inevitably impact not just the greatness of leadership that emerges but also the quality of products and the improvements, based on research and innovativeness, that can be achieved. In the next chapter, that is what our focus must be on.

CHAPTER 7

IMPACT OF LOCATION
ON LEADERSHIP

Could Oprah Winfrey have emerged a leading TV personality in the USA if it were not for that land's democratic and *free-market* nature? Could Jack Ma have built an empire in China had he not benefited from starting his journey to the top in the USA? Could the Issa brothers, magnates in the UK's petroleum industry, have leapt to the top had they lived in Guatemala or Cuba? The answer to those questions is possibly, but highly unlikely. Why? Because location matters.

In this chapter, we want to delve into the matter of location and how it affects leadership. Not many have given thought to the fact that location matters because it seems like such a hopeless thing to think about. However, those who wish to start a business will want to locate it where all the elements required to make it flourish are *congregated*. It does not make sense, for instance, to set up a company designed to go global in a place like Cuba or Chile – the political and social atmospheres there just will not enable it.

We are intent on unraveling the nature of political governance and prevailing socio-economic patterns on the overall leadership styles in a nation or region in the next few pages. Our goal is to demonstrate that superior leadership is a factor of a set of conditions both within oneself and some that are obviously without – elements controlled by the political process and the pace at which social life evolved in a given land.

The North-South divide and geopolitics have made it seem that nations to the north are better run and experience more stable environments where leadership and growth flourish, while nations to the south experience the reverse. Africa and South America are lumped up among continents where growth is stifled by the nature of political leadership and governance styles involved. In the so-called northern divide, most Western nations are run based on policies and statutes that enhance a friendlier business environment.

To gain an understanding of the corrosive impact of political philosophies and ideologies on the quality of leadership a nation enjoys – in the business, religious, academic, and even military life – one has to examine the nature of governance styles like democracy, socialism, authoritarianism and military rule. It is upon understanding these core governance styles that we may be able to tell, with certainty, why certain regions of the world have excelled in leadership and have forged ahead in business and social cohesion. In contrast, others have remained stuck in a mindset that discourages free thought, industry, and competitiveness in ideas and scale of productivity.

Democracy

We will not dwell on a rigid history of democracy as a form of governance other than to say it was the Greeks who gave it to the world. Democracy has since been described as a rule of the people, by the people, and for the people. Universal suffrage is at the core of it. Leaders are elected by the vote of each citizen and are held to account for their actions ever so often – four years being common.

Having experimented with other forms of governance, the world settled on democracy as the most favorable for humankind. Most of the Western world – led by the USA and Britain – got in the act and adopted democracy and free-market economics. Ideologies that would not only free citizens to pursue excellence in individual pursuits but would eventually create vibrant and perfecting societies where growth is pegged on the ability of the nations to keep on a path to the pursuit of greater freedoms and innovation.

It shouldn't come as a surprise that in a duopolistic world, where the USSR and the USA competed for ideological supremacy, the USSR championing communism, and the USA democracy, the USA won the race and has since remained the sole superpower in the world. China, often described by modern Chinese leaders as a "socialist democracy," is now on the ascendancy, but it is somewhat of an anomaly. The former leader of the People's Republic of China, Deng Xiaoping, once famously said, "What does it matter what is the color of the cat provided it catches mice."

Democracy, by its nature, creates open societies where leaders and citizens are freed to be creative, innovative, and are rewarded for coming up with bold new ideas. Democratic governance generates an atmosphere where the goal is excellence and the drive to maximization of output is celebrated and not vilified. In a democracy, each position is held by a competent official because the atmosphere is geared toward rewarding only the best.

The key features in a democracy, which enhance an atmosphere of winning, are:

a. Competitiveness. Whether in elections or in picking a leader for a company, votes are cast after each candidate has been given a fair chance to articulate their issues. Through the voting process, one of the candidates is elected, purely to lead the nation or company toward greater *successes*. Such success is defined in:

- Quality of life of the people – longer life expectancy, higher income, drop in the number of uninsured citizens, and even a more educated populace.

- Respectability. In a nation, respect is earned based on the GDP, a rise in production, anchored on greater and sustainable wealth-creation, and core regard on the global stage. In a company, respect is earned based on innovativeness leading to maximum productivity, a larger market share, and leadership in new product lines.

- Sustainability. It is not enough that a leader may emerge who performs a miracle that will not be replicated in another nation or company. Success is achieved when a solid foundation is laid, upon which future leaders will keep a company building to grow even further for the betterment of everyone.

b. Free flow of thought. Whether in a nation or a company, a free flow of thought is critical to success. Leaders and workers must feel part of the process by airing their views on aspects of production, leadership, supply chain, and any new idea that may pop up in the course of work. Only when a vibrant exchange of ideas is enabled can an entity be assured of sustaining its walk to dominance.

c. Accountability. Leaders are expected to live up to their promises (word) or be asked to step aside. Every four or five years, nations hold their leaders to account by reelecting them or firing them. In most companies, similarly, boards are constituted to hold a leader to account. It boils down to three factors:

- Profits. Has the company's portfolio expanded, and are the dividends to shareholders reflective of growth?

- Imaging. What is the perception of the company in the public eye? Is the company regarded as a friend or a foe in the community it serves?

- Fidelity to vision. A nation or a company may be profitable and even enjoy a wonderful perception in the host community. Still, if that is all that is achieved outside the scope of the vision it is supposed to move toward, it is time to take corrective measures − since profits must not become the *ultimate* measure of success.

d. Graceful handover. Democratic nations and the organizations in them have matured in this area. After a vote, the winner graciously declares victory and the loser concedes defeat. This is made possible because:

- The process is credible. Elections in most Western nations are credible, and people view them as such. Thus, when one is defeated in an election, they graciously bow out.

- It is about *ideas*. Democracy revolves around ideas and not personalities. If one is elected, it is a testament to the quality of ideas offered; if one is not elected, it is because the ideas they put across fell short. Thus, no one regards a loss as a *personal* thing; it is the weak ideas that have been rejected.

- Second chances. Defeat in one election is not the end of the road. One can run a second or a third and even a fourth time as long as they believe that the ideas they have are better suited to take the nation or company to the next level.

It would be a disservice to fail to mention that in a democracy, a free press, an assertive legislature, an independent judiciary, and a restrained executive are key to vibrancy. *Institutionalization* of a nation's constitution is what makes it a stable democracy, governed by the rule of law and enabled to seek a place at the table of sister nations, where citizens are free to work, worship, play, and think only in accordance with conscience and in fidelity to the letter and spirit of the constitution.

Authoritarianism

Authoritarian nations tend to be either in sub-Saharan Africa or in South America. They happen to be nations where the rule of law is suspended, and a strongman is in total control. In Africa, they are also called dictatorships. The tragedy is that such nations have entrenched this manner of rule in the constitution and have cowered citizens into toeing the line or be killed, maimed, or charged in a kangaroo court, where a conviction is assured.

Unlike in a democracy, decision-making in a rabid authoritarian state is top-down. No one dares to say a word before the word of the big man is heard and digested. Once it is heard, whether right or wrong, it is repeated with gusto, everyone eager to please the boss and stay safe – because opposition may mean an assassination or other forms of gory intimidation. Fear is the order of the day here.

Strangely, even in authoritarian states, strongmen have their supporters, men and women who are beneficiaries of their misrules. In North Korea, the supreme ruler has rallied a weary nation toward his bombastic policies by threat, intimidation, and the elimination of opposition. In much of Africa, the new strongmen have perfected the art of pretense to hold democratic elections, yet the outcome of such charades is never in doubt. Hitler too had his core supporters and built an empire by the sheer force of terror and an uncanny ability to rally a nation to his incredulous policies.

Naturally, a nation run through authoritarianism is not expected to produce leaders of the kind democratic nations produce. Here, leaders are not in their important positions based on competence or professionalism but based on nepotism, tribalism, cronyism, and many times on the supreme leader's raw word. With a network of informants and spies, leaders at all levels – in the government or the private sector – are not to be heard taking a position on a matter until the word has come from the top.

Authoritarianism comes in three forms:

a. Dictatorships. A nation may begin its long walk as a democracy, but it may eventually elect a leader who has no regard for the tenets of democracy and may wish to hang on to power. Such a leader will ultimately lead the nation down a path to dictatorship by a blatant disregard for the rule of law. It may take a minute for the impact of such a trend to catch on, but eventually, it does, and leaders at all levels and in all sectors suffer the lack of participatory governance.

b. Military juntas. The West African nation of Nigeria experienced life under a military junta when General Sani Abacha came to power through the barrel of a gun. Like in authoritarian nations, decision-making is top-down and is rigid. Leaders in the key sectors are placed under an *overseer* military commander and are expected to act only after hearing from them.

c. Hermit kingdoms. North Korea is a prime example of a hermit kingdom. A closed system under which it maintains its isolation even from its closest neighbors and allies. Strict adherence to discipline that runs top-down is the only way to avoid repercussions; thus, leadership is of pitifully low quality and cannot measure up to global standards.

Authoritarianism stands for everything democracy is against – no free press, a flower-girl legislative arm, a shamelessly dependent judiciary, and an imperial presidency or executive. In an atmosphere like that, leadership cannot grow. There is only one center of thought. Decisions are made by a coterie of powerful yes men and women dedicated only to self-preservation and continued indulgence.

The reason authoritarianism is unable to nurture competent leadership is because of the fruits the system bears. It creates men and women unable to stand on their own by thinking independently and demonstrating an ability to be innovative.

Where authoritarianism has taken hold, therefore, what is to be expected is:

a. Fear. The fear of making wrong decisions, acting out of turn, facing dire consequences, and the general unpredictability of the times makes it impossible for anyone to dare to think or dream big. People must wait to be told what to do, eliminating personal initiative and the drive for excellence.

b. Lethargy. Due to a lack of drive, it is not a surprise that people begin to get laidback and act only when they must – and even then, work in a halfhearted manner.

c. Intense mistrust. In a police state or a company run based on authoritarianism, people tend to distrust others. Informants are generally never known, thus creating an atmosphere where suspicion runs rampant.

d. Decay. There should be no surprise that at the end of the day, a system operated based on fear will decay. A nation where renewal never happens and a company where free thought is stifled eventually fails in its core role of innovation and faces decay on a level that ultimately leads to collapse.

e. Implosion. The USSR imploded. Rwanda imploded, too. In South America, several nations have faced revolutions. By nature, humans are born to be free. When a system is created that binds them and stifles free thought, it will *eventually* decay and implode.

Socialism

Socialism is a system of governance where the state controls all means of production, and wealth is shared equally. On paper, this is supposed to be a great system, one where everyone is well taken care of, but it has *failed* to live up to its billing in reality. Why? Because of human nature – selfishness.

In socialist nations like Tanzania, Cuba, and the former USSR, where leaders experimented with this form of governance, it failed to catch on. They later shifted gears to free-market economics and the pursuit of individual enterprise because growth was discovered to have its root in *human selfishness*. An enterprise was going to grow only because the owner put in the effort for his or her sake, not for others' sake. It was all about *mine*!

Thus, socialism created leaders with a willingness to work for the good of everyone, but for the most part, the element of communal ownership caused several leaders *not* to give it their very best. Leaders were created whose drive was stifled by the fact that there was not much to draw from the effort. Thus, though socialism was a far better system of governance than dictatorship or authoritarianism, it faced the same challenge where it concerned the creation of leaders dedicated and able to compete with others on the global stage. Not surprisingly, it was not long before socialist nations faced the prospect of decay, and most eventually imploded, leaving in their wake, leaders ready to change course and embrace democracy.

Culture

Once again, the North-South divide comes into play on this subject matter. We have established that most governments in the northern hemisphere are run based on democracy and have developed leaders ready for the complexities of the twenty-first century. On the other hand, the southern hemisphere has given the world incompetent leaders due to governance systems inspired by the policies of dictators, authoritarians, and military rulers. At this point, we want to find out how the same North-South divide has affected culture and how that culture has affected leadership.

Culture is the prevailing way of life of a people, an accepted standard of life with regulations, laws, and norms that are enforceable by the leadership of a given place. Whether in worship, dressing, eating, education, law and order, and other critical elements of life, the definer of it all is culture. The culture of a locality is a reflection of the kind of governance structure it follows. Do not expect democracy to produce a culture of social stratification, as is the case in monarchies. Do not expect an authoritarian government to produce a culture of tolerance and innovation. That is not real life.

Culture has been identified as a critical determinant of the kind of leadership a locality or region will produce. In India, where the culture of a caste system has been in place for so long, there is a class of citizens who will never rise from the lowest castes to lead an enterprise or the nation. The caste system is a natural dehumanizer that condemns one to a lifelong state of destitution because of its insistence on a stratified society – created so by the gods!

In Africa – on the other hand – a rich culture has been weaved around the concept of patriarchy and taboos. Leaders are expected to be men – both at home and in public. Men are expected to be strong and wise. To this effect, taboos have been built around social expectations, where women are to be seen but not heard. It is evident that Africa, like most places in the world, is making efforts to leave this mindset behind, but it still lingers. Where it is strong, women leaders are a token and are not taken seriously – at least not as seriously as their male counterparts. The impact of such a culture on leadership cannot be gainsaid; it denies Africa the ability to create an atmosphere where women can rise to the top on merit.

In closing this chapter, it is important to point out that the geographical region one lives in will play a critical role in shaping the nature of leadership one will offer. This is an important factor to consider as one is gearing up to establish an enterprise or decide which nation to immigrate to. If you care deeply about human freedom, it does not make sense to immigrate to Guatemala or Nepal; it makes better sense to immigrate to the USA or the United Kingdom.

A visionary, one whose goal is to create a product that will impact the globe, does well to locate his or her enterprise in a developed democracy like the United States of America, Japan, or the emerging superpower, China. The nature of governance and the culture it fosters is critical to the kind of leaders a nation or region will offer. That will, in turn, have a significant impact on the ability of a vision to embrace a global outreach or shrink into a local venture. The world would have never heard of Jack Ma had he not moved to the USA, where his skills and drive were going to be supported by a vibrant market defined by aggressive innovation, freedom, and a system of governance that allowed citizens to work hard for a commensurate reward.

It is easy to tell, after that geopolitical discussion, why the Western world has accommodated and encouraged the emergence of the thoughtful Zen leader as opposed to the southern hemispheric nations, which have tended to create more of the authoritarian Alpha leaders. Geographical location matters and is a key determinant of the nature of leadership a region experiences. It also speaks to the kind of business venture and scope of vision one may entertain in the locality.

In the next chapter, we turn our attention to *models of leadership*. In leadership, there are several models one may rely on to achieve results. Though each model of choice will depend on several factors, we are about to find out that the leading question one must ask before deciding to lead at all is – *who in the world am I?* We are talking about identity.

Identity plays a fundamental role in the nature of leadership one has to offer. Therefore, the question we seek to answer is – can a leader depart from his or her core identity and adopt a leadership model outside the range of who they are and still become successful? Can one born with the natural tendencies of accommodative leadership flip to become authoritarian?

Can we go from Zen to Alpha leadership instead of Alpha to Zen leadership?

CHAPTER 8

MODELS IN LEADERSHIP

As we have discussed trends in modern leadership, it is easy to have imagined that for a great leader to emerge in the twenty-first century, there can only be one formula—just one model. Whereas there are evident character traits associated with greatness in leadership in all the celebrated leaders of the past and present times, leadership styles have varied. In Mandela, we see pragmatic, adaptable leadership. In Hitler, we see dictatorial leadership. In Jack Ma, we see participative leadership. In Elon Musk, we see achievement-oriented leadership. Therefore, the question we seek to grapple with is what *determines* the leadership model or models best adaptable for a particular nation or company?

The truth is – the kind of person one is plays the most critical role in creating the leader they are to become eventually. One's core identity in the realm of character, disposition, and temperament is a key player in deciding how issues presented to them will be received and adjudicated. That said, several other factors will play a role in the type of leadership an entity needs to grow.

Before we delve deeper into the nature of leadership models the world has witnessed, it is crucial to understand the special elements that predispose a given entity to work best with one approach and not another in leadership.

a. Nature of company. This is a crucial *decider* of the kind of leadership an entity requires to match its needs. When an entity happens to have a leadership style that mismatches its essential character, the entity inevitably suffers and may later implode if the danger of decay is not immediately solved. When we talk of nature, we explore aspects like:

- Is it a global operation? A global concern like DHL or Coca-Cola cannot be offered the kind of leadership a regional chain or a national institution is offered. A leader hired to guide the affairs of a multinational concern must be of a given disposition.

- Is it a national institution? Most nations have companies that are set up within their borders and serve only a national clientele. It is important to match those organizations with leadership capable of handling matters of a national scope to satisfy all stakeholders in the venture.

- Military. Can the military afford a procrastinator or a laissez-faire leadership? Can it do well with a leader ignorant about global and regional affairs? The answer is *no*. This is an entity that requires proactive leadership and needs an intelligent mind at the top.

- Church. Because of its nature as an agent of *salvation*, the church needs a gentle leader that acts like a shepherd. Commands and bluster are not an approach that will serve the entity well.

- Gender-based institutions. They are to be run by women if they cater to the needs of women or by men if they cater to men's needs. The leadership offered here must be tailor-made to fit the specific needs of the entity.

b. Location. The location of a company or nation determines the nature of leadership it requires. A nation like the USA, billing itself as the leader of global democracy, can only be led by a man or woman whose *philosophical* predisposition is in tune with human freedoms. A company in North Korea can only attract subservient leadership, uninventive, and not at all ready to rock the boat. The location of an entity determines the nature of the leader it can live with.

c. Culture. Culture is like *a box*. It allows those who subscribe to a given range of social, economic and political tenets to live within the confines of the box. Naturally, leaders within a given culture will tend to be a reflection of the values and boundaries they impose on the people. For example, some of the liberal views a British leader lauds at home, a leader in Uganda cannot. Talk of issues like gay rights can happen in the context of broader human freedoms in the West, not in Africa. Leaders in these contexts, thus, must reflect those peculiar realities and emerge from within those contexts.

Jeff Bezos, the founder of Amazon, the giant retail chain, began his work in the basement of his home, never imagining it would end up becoming the behemoth it has. With an unparalleled dedication, supported by his brilliant wife, McKenzie, he exploited the elements within a democratic, business-friendly America to build one of the world's largest retail stores.

A recluse, rarely seen in public, those interested in studying business models have attempted to get to the bottom of the model that has worked for the Amazon chief, but it appears to remain a work in progress. Regardless, the business has grown to the extent that it was instantly regarded as the largest divorce settlement in history when Jeff and McKenzie recently divorced.

I believe it is probably not helpful to attach the label of a specific leadership model to a given leader. If anything, there will be broader or essential characters of a certain style in a leader. Still, there will also be moments when occasions require that a leader acts outside the box of their *expected* range of behavior. Thus, the approach we need to adopt in this discussion is not what was Mandela's style or Obama's style, or Oprah's, but what are the manifesting models in leadership and how do they affect productivity? What are their characteristics, and how do the subjects respond to them? Because of the nature of my consultancy, where I have done exceedingly well with participative leadership, that is the model I want to begin with.

Participative Leadership

This is the kind of leadership where the leader is *predisposed* to rigorous and meaningful consultations with employees and all management levels to seek their suggestions and take their ideas into serious consideration before decisions are made. It is the kind of leadership one might call democratic, except that it goes far deeper than democracy. It purposefully places workers at all levels of a company at the center of its operations.

The legendary Jack Welch – at the helm of the Michigan-based General Electric for decades – was a master of participative leadership. The giant corporation had unionized and contractual employees, and all felt motivated to give their best because of the nature of leadership Jack offered. He made the janitor feel just as key to the corporation's success as the mid and top-level managers. By the time Welch retired from General Electric, the corporation had steadily emerged into one of America's brightest examples – no wonder those he led didn't want to let him go!

Thus, the question one may ask is what makes a participative leader such an asset to a company?

a. Worker morale. People know and feel it when they are treated well. Being treated well revolves around:

- Offering employees the opportunity for development.

- Seeking and acting fully on employee feedback.

- Showing genuine appreciation and celebrating accomplishments.

- Offering competitive benefits and compensation.

- Empowering employees to give their very best.

It is only when worker morale is high that a company's productivity and profit margins will rise. Participative leadership boosts morale because it shares the company's successes and failures with everyone – complete ownership of results is the cornerstone of operations in such a venture.

b. Harmony. A culture of a harmonious drive during production is essential to success. It reduces conflict issues, which inevitably deny managers time to focus on production as human resource issues are solved.

c. Competitiveness. A participative leadership style can enhance productivity and usher in *the competitiveness* of a company's products. The highest point in a leader's career should be when they hear all workers – from the lowest to the highest ranked – take full ownership of successes by declaring, "This is how *we* do it!" That is the mark of participative leadership.

Achievement-oriented Leadership

This leadership is not as warm as the participative style. It is warm and agreeable when results are being achieved but can become *tough* and carelessly demanding when that is not the case. In a way, it relies on a bit of dictatorship to thrive.

If you ask whether there is any leader who does not seek to achieve results, the answer is yes and no. Yes, because every leader wants to achieve results; no, because leaders will not go

117

for those results if they conflict with certain values. The ruthlessness that drives achievement-oriented leaders – making them go for results at whatever cost to self and company – is what sets them apart from leaders with self-restraint. We call this the "Win at all costs" mentality.

A better understanding of leaders of this nature is only possible when we delve into the *characteristics* evidenced by their actions:

a. They expect their employees to perform at their highest levels unfailingly. The issues of illnesses, family problems, or any such intrusive matters are frowned upon. Work is the only matter that counts, even if the leader may pretend otherwise.

b. They always seek improvement in employee performance. The employee is regarded as a machine that must be serviced and made to perform at an optimum level. The employee is not engineered to improve performance for his or her betterment but for the good of the company.

c. They show a high degree of confidence in employee accountability and responsibility. This is because they are confident in the drill regimen that has produced the worker in question. Thus, they do not doubt that an employee will accomplish even complex tasks –

because the employee has been trained to think and act a certain way.

Achievement-oriented leadership produces results and may even seem successful, and often thrives in an environment where workers have no other choices of competing companies to work for. People want to feel wanted, respected, and appreciated. Workers will naturally gravitate toward an atmosphere where *respect* abounds. That is the downside achievement-oriented leadership must grapple with – to put humanity above huge profits, product lines, and market share.

Laissez-faire Leadership

Laissez-faire leadership is primarily based on trust. Individuals who prefer a lot of independence in making decisions and do their best work when working autonomously are often comfortable with a laissez-faire leader. From this leader's perspective, the key to success is to build a team of experts and then leave them to get on with it. Laissez-faire is a French term that translates as "leave alone." With this type of leadership style, leaders largely leave it up to their team to complete tasks and projects in a method of their choosing, without the need for strict policies and procedures. It should be noted, however, that laissez-faire leadership does not fit every company or environment. I would go as far as to say that while it is true that some companies thrive under laissez-faire leaders, this style of leadership is not suited to most companies.

In a company where this nature of leadership manifests, there will be clear indications of aspects of operations leaning a certain way:

a. Drive. Self-starters with a drive to succeed work effectively under laissez-faire leaders as they do not have the ongoing need to be told what to do.

b. Authority. Leaders delegate authority to their capable experts. They develop and make the best use of their staff's leadership qualities but are ready to step in in a crisis. Staff are expected to anticipate problems, identify opportunities, and are given the authority to pivot if needed.

c. Reward. They motivate staff to perform at their optimum level, monitor results, praise achievements, and reward successes.

d. Challenge. They offer constructive challenges, encourage staff to solve problems, manage and mitigate risk, and take personal responsibility for their failures.

Because of their hands-off philosophy, people often misinterpret laissez-faire leaders as having a lack of focus, drive, an understanding of what the company is there to achieve and occupy an office of power and influence – mostly for prestige and the trappings of glory it confers on one. It is true when laissez-faire leadership is misused, such as in cases where the team lacks adequate skills and experience, it can create more problems than it solves, resulting in a lack of accountability within the team or company and a failure to achieve goals.

I will leave you with famous quotes from leaders who are widely regarded as having embodied at least in part, laissez-faire leadership.

Ronald Reagan: "Surround yourself with the best people you can find, delegate authority, and don't interfere as long as the policy you've decided upon is being carried out."

Warren Buffett: "Pick out associates whose behavior is better than yours, and you'll drift in that direction."

Andrew Mellon: "Strong men have sound ideas and the force to make these ideas effective."

Donna Karan: "I design from instinct. It's the only way I know how to live. What feels good. What feels right. What is needed. Give me a problem, and I will approach it creatively, from my gut."

Pragmatic Leadership

This kind of leadership, arguably, encompasses all manner of leaderships. A pragmatic leader is ready and able to be participative, a delegator; become laissez-faire, dictatorial, and even a procrastinator – it depends on what the immediate circumstances call for. This leader does not allow themself to be boxed into rigid patterns that deny one the ability to innovate and implement new solutions.

A pragmatic leader is defined by:

a. Proactivity. They think about a matter before it has become a problem. The ability to foresee opportunities or problems is of great importance – but to act ahead of time to solve them is even more important. In certain instances, such a leader solves core problems, and his team may never become aware that the leader averted a potential crisis without their input.

b. Intellectual rigor. Unlike the laissez-faire leader, this leader reads prolifically, thinks a lot, and may even be a significant contributor to prevailing thought through leading business publications. Such a leader is regarded as a trend-setter, an authoritative voice on topical matters in the field.

c. Decisiveness. The ability to quickly weigh a situation through data and other evidence is key to pragmatism.

A leader in this mold can make quick decisions and live with them – taking full responsibility for all outcomes associated with the decision. In the person of Barack Obama, the United States of America gave the world such a leader, a sharp pragmatist who took full responsibility for the multiplicity of decisions and actions of his two-term administration.

d. Results-orientation. Pragmatism inevitably leads to results. The guiding philosophy is to move the company or nation in the direction of achieving goals and objectives. If profits look great and clear data is available to demonstrate growth in all the aspects of operations, a pragmatist is happy.

We have taken a look at some leading models of leadership. It is clear that we lean one way or another on these core models, but it would be better if we could switch between models as necessary. Pragmatism makes us leaders whose followers can count on because they know we are able to think outside the box, innovate and boldly implement ideas. They know a pragmatist will consult, will be dictatorial, and may even be a procrastinator – but all for the good of the company. It is all about trust and confidence in the nobility and established character of the leader.

In the next chapter, we are turning our attention to the important matter of *mentorship*. A leader's role is not entirely played until they have identified and trained those who will step into their leadership role when choosing to retire or move on to another position. Greatness in leadership is, indeed, defined by the wisdom to fundamentally shape the future by nurturing continuity through mentorship. Great leaders do not pull up the ladder behind them.

Therefore, the question we seek to answer is — is it the place of the current leader to influence what will happen after they are gone, or should the leader allow whoever comes next to veer a company or a nation in whatever direction they wish? Is it the leader's place to set an entity or nation on a path to Zen leadership or the path determined by an Alpha leader?

CHAPTER 9

MENTORSHIP

We have covered a lot of ground in the preceding chapters. A clear image is forming about what it takes to become a great leader. Leadership, though, is not just about what one accomplishes when in a leadership position, but what they do to keep the train of success on the rail even after leaving the scene.

There have been those who have argued that once one has departed a scene, events will naturally lean away from their trajectory. In a way, that is indeed inevitable. We have already discussed that the only permanent object in this world is change – and in the twenty-first-century, changes are many, aggressive and unsettling. Therefore, whatever any leader leaves behind will soon be cast aside by the powerful forces of change, they say.

It is an understandable position to take, but it is also a position that denies the reality of continuity and releases a company or a nation into the hands of men and women without the skills, temperament, zeal, and loyalty to its vision. It is to say I do not care what happens after me – let the next leader struggle to figure it out the best they can. That is irresponsible and cannot be viewed as leadership, no matter how well one did at the helm. Continuity is paramount. So, what does it mean to mentor someone?

Defining Mentorship

Mentorship is the act of walking one through a process with the aim of making the person gain critical knowledge in the operational procedures of a company – even a nation. The importance of mentoring cannot be overstated. A well-managed mentorship strategy should be implemented as part of succession planning. Zen leaders are acutely aware of this need; Alpha ones carry on as if they will be around forever.

One of the most successful mentorships the world has witnessed recently was Apple's smooth transition from the distressing death of the founder and brains behind the operations, Steve Jobs. At the time of his death, when he made the profound statement that the sickbed was the most expensive bed there was, he had trained Tim Cook in all the ways of the company, and the man was ready to carry on the winning ways that had made Apple a force in the industry.

In one BBC interview, when Cook was asked what had made him remain on the path to success with Apple, he pointed to the foundation Steve Jobs had laid and the fact that he kept the company on the same path his predecessor had started it on. It was based on staying the course that Apple kept growing and managed to keep competitors in the rearview mirror, unable to cut into the impressive market share Apple had carved for itself under the stewardship of the departed innovator and tech mogul of the twenty-first century.

Thus, a mentor can only be defined by the nature of the mentees they leave behind. Identifying the mentees is a matter that begins reasonably early – at a time a leader has determined that they won't be in the company for long either due to retirement, illness, transfer, or the need to move on to a different line of engagement. The questions one needs to ask in the process of identifying the mentees are:

a. Is the individual personable? It is based on temperament and people skills that one can be judged either personable or not. It is imperative that a leader spot that talent as early as possible to nurture it to eventually pass the baton.

b. Is the individual of high intellect? It does not help to leave a company or a nation in the hands of a person who lacks curiosity and is bereft of intellectual gravitas. In this bold, new century, the only way one leads an operation successfully, is if they can positively interact with the complex and rapidly changing nature of issues on the global and national stage. A leader picking a mentee must take this into account.

c. Is the individual astute? Some have called an astute individual street smart. It matters little, though, what label one uses; what we are referring to here is an individual able to grapple with problematic situations and apply solutions that will ultimately lead to resolution and growth from one level to the next.

d. Is the individual time-conscious? A leader understands the true value of time. A notoriously late leader cannot be relied on to lead any entity to success and is not to be mentored for leadership. Anyone who cannot manage their time demonstrates the regard they have for an assignment – the kind of regard that will translate into low productivity and low staff morale.

e. Is the individual industrious? Of course, hard work goes along with working smart to meet deadlines, reach goals, and exceed expectations in deliverables.

The character traits mentioned above should guide the company in identifying potential future leaders. At the end of the day, people will judge one based on the kind of new leaders they have left behind. That is what mentorship boils down to – *taking care of the future today*!

Trust and Guidance

As in several nations, the American presidency is designed to be occupied by a president and a vice president. At the end of a term, the vice president is usually expected to run for office to replace their outgoing boss. Naturally, the two leaders must work closely to ensure that the missteps of their time in office do not negatively affect the vice president and complicate their election bid.

A leader who is ready to mentor someone must cultivate trust and be willing to selflessly offer great advice, guidance, and act as the explainer-in-chief on all matters a company or nation faces. Despite Vice President Joe Biden being a senior to the newly elected president, Barack Obama, Joe was keen to learn from Barack, and Barack was willing to trust his vice president fully.

In the election of 2020, four years after Barack had left the White House to Donald Trump, the new president, the mentorship paid off when Joe Biden was nominated by the Democratic Party to run for president and carry on the legacy of the Obama-Biden administration.

In a century when changes are rapid, and there's a far greater demand on one's time than ever before, it takes a lot of patience to mentor someone. Trust and the willingness to offer guidance can only be nurtured in an atmosphere where key elements can flourish:

a. Role modeling. It takes place when a leader acts with the mentee in mind, mindful that the mentee is studiously observing each word and action. Role modeling is the most *effective* way to mentor an individual. It cuts out words, pretenses, and goes to the heart of the matter – this is how it's done. Those who have been modeled by a great leader often become great as casts in the same role.

b. Affirmations and corrections *devoid* of grim putdowns. A role model must be mindful of the feelings of a mentee. It makes a huge difference when one is affirmed, praised, or encouraged after doing things right. It also makes a difference when one is corrected in a spirit of love and care – to enhance the element of trust and bonding. No one will ever learn well under duress. Thus, affirmations and corrections must be viewed as elements in building trust and as acts geared toward building capacity in a mentee.

c. Allowing tagalongs. The quickest manner to learn is when one can tag along with the leader – to experience a situation in real-time and observe how the leader handles it. Leaders who deny mentees this experience deny them a critical tool in *practical learning* and may eventually produce theorists rather than hands-on experts. It would indeed be even more impactful if when the mentees tagalong, they are cast in the practical role of the leader to make crucial decisions and take ownership of them whether things go well or blow up in their faces.

Bill Gates has gone around the world, mentoring a new crop of entrepreneurs. Jack Ma has done the same through his business school. Oprah Winfrey has invested heavily in a school of excellence in South Africa to mentor the continent's future leaders. No company or political figure can lay claim to successful leadership without leaving in place, disciples capable of carrying on where they have left off. Indeed, one fundamental way to judge a leader's success is to assess how an entity they led has performed post their departure.

One of the reasons South Africa has held steady after the death of Nelson Mandela is because the leader mentored several youthful men who were ready to step in when he parted. There was Thabo Mbeki, Jacob Zuma, Cyril Ramaphosa, and a couple of others. The nation was going to face a shortage of capable leaders because of Mandela's death. That is what mentorship is about. He prepared South Africa for his exit through his words and actions and ensured the leaders he molded into great men would follow in his footsteps.

Once fresh leaders have been generated through mentorship, however, the way a baton is passed is the next important factor. Mandela ensured that he set South Africa on a path to democracy and left one of his core mentees in charge

– in a peaceful election and transfer of power. In 2020, Obama worked to help his mentee, Joe Biden, win a presidential race and expand the policies they started. It matters how a leader passes that baton. It can be passed in a way that grows the company or nation, or it can be passed in a manner that all but ensures the company will never remain on a path to prosperity. Wise leadership calls on a great leader to do three important things as they pass the baton:

- Paint the vision afresh. The danger of a new leader departing from the current vision is an ever-present danger in companies. It is a danger in nations as well. Before he retired, Mandela called his political sons and painted the vision of the nation he had in mind afresh. He extolled the virtues of democracy and racial harmony, then told them to live up to that calling. He famously said, "Don't call me, I'll call you" on the day he bowed out – that was after he was sure the vision was locked in their hearts. Not to paint a vision afresh is to set a new captain in the seas without a picture of the place or a way to get to that destination.

- Explain the historical journey. This involves recounting the walk from the beginning to the present and using that model to draw a future picture. Tell the mentees who started the journey, where they began the journey, who they were with, where they intended to go, and how far they have come. At the time of passing the baton, this skill is important. The new leaders need to have a clear understanding of what they are inheriting and how it must connect its past to its future to succeed.

- Fall into the role of overseer. As the day draws close to depart, a leader must recede into the background and play the role of *overseer*. At this point, the role should be limited to offering advice, inspiration, and ensuring that the mentee can run the affairs of the company or nation when they are gone. Some leaders find it hard to let go, to pull back from the day-to-day running of an entity. There is a selfish tendency in that approach. A leader who is not keen on letting mentees assume more significant roles is not confident about the quality of leaders they have helped to mold.

Let us close this chapter with the powerful story of the founder of Ford Motors Corporation. Henry Ford was a Michigan entrepreneur who envisioned a new way to build cars and went out of his way to pursue the dream. He painted such a clear vision of his dream that successive leaders after he was gone were able to explain it and mentor others to keep on the path to innovation and successes so far achieved by the company.

Nearly a century after its founding, the Ford Motor Corporation remains a dominant force in the car production industry and a giant market share controller in America and the world. It comes down to how its successive leaders have been mentored through the years and how they have internalized the vision Henry Ford had when he founded the giant corporation – today, an employer of thousands of Americans and a key investor in markets beyond the borders of the USA.

Once again, it goes without saying that in nations steeped in entrenched democratic practices and good governance, the element of mentorship is far more robust than in dictatorships and in military-run governments. Free societies tend to generate more space for leaders to move on to different fields or retirement because opportunities abound that one may move on to. Thus, such societies activate an atmosphere where seasoned leaders are willing and able to mentor younger ones to take their place. That is classic Zen leadership. In dictatorships, the exact opposite is the case. Since opportunities are limited, leaders are neither willing nor are eager to mentor the young, *fearing* that they will be replaced before they are ready to step aside for younger blood. That is an Alpha leader's thought process.

Succession is important. It is unfailingly established by the element we have discussed in this chapter – that being mentorship. Any company that fails to address the matter of mentorship will struggle. Any leader who fails to mentor successors ensures that his or her legacy will amount to nothing. Jack Ma has established his legacy by mentoring others through his business school in China. Oprah Winfrey has secured her legacy by founding a futuristic school of excellence in South Africa. Bill Gates has done the same by starting a foundation that champions values he holds dear to his heart. The ongoing mentorship in these key institutions guarantees that the vision these leaders painted will live on.

Unfortunately, and perhaps in equal measure, the vilest leaders history has produced have also left a legacy behind. Hitler left a legacy of ruin, division, and a ruinous war whose impact the world is still dealing with today. Pol Pot so terrorized Cambodia that his name remains locked up in the annals of the world's darkest *history* to this day. It is a blessing that those they mentored were later defeated, and those who have admired their despicable approach to leadership have dismally failed to catch traction in a world determined to drive humanity in the general direction of tolerance, togetherness, and a commonsense approach to governance.

In the next chapter, we are turning our attention to the matter of legacy. No leader wants to get off the stage of life and not be remembered for what they did while on earth. Therefore, the question we seek to answer is – should anyone be focused on how history will judge them by having one eye on the present and another in the deep future as they execute roles today?

CHAPTER 10

LEGACY

The question we are setting out to answer in this chapter is a fundamental one. At this point, a leader is coming to terms with the fact that they will not always be around – and begin to worry about how history will judge actions, words, trends, and failures attributed to them. In the USA, former leaders have built presidential libraries to further shape their legacy and define them a certain way to future generations. Not a bad idea. But at what time should a leader shape their legacy? When is it most impactful to get on the wheel to shaping a legacy?

The place to *begin* a discussion on this fundamental question is *at birth*. Often, we make the silly mistake of thinking that a leader just emerged on the world stage and became who they are due to circumstances unassociated with their formative years and state of affairs at birth. The truth is our upbringing plays a foundational role in what we will become and, thus, is the first shaper of our legacy.

Among the Jews, there is the belief that a child's character is formed by the time they turn *eight*. The traits and strength of character that will manifest later in the child's life are displayed when they are just eight years old. If anything is to be done to steer the child away from destructive tendencies, that is the time to do it; otherwise, the traits on display slowly crystalize into core character and live on in the child's life – a way of life or habit.

The trouble with habit is that it endures. Once it is formed, it takes a lot of effort to unlearn it. Indeed, consider the word itself – HABIT. If you remove the H, you still have ABIT of it left. If you remove the A, you still have BIT of it left. If you remove the B, you still have IT left. And if you remove the I, you still have the T left to remind you of the scars acquired when it was a habit. This illustration is meant to awaken us to the reality that our legacy begins its shaping earlier than most of us think.

In most detective thrillers and crime scene shows, psychoanalysts usually go in-depth in drawing out the real character of an offender and the core motivations that triggered the unwanted behavior. In most cases, those triggers turn out to be associated with a childhood or an upbringing situation that left the offender affected negatively and began the slide toward the day of committing the crime. That the offender would later be characterized as a *criminal* or deviant is a drawn-out process that started way before they began to manifest the character in question. In essence, we are saying that like the criminal, the legacy of a leader begins to shape up way back in the leader's childhood – the formative years.

Legacy Defined

So, what is legacy? I will depart from the standard definition you might encounter in a dictionary or a thesaurus. Based on a broader *interpretation* of one's life, legacy is the totality of actions and words of a given individual and how they have affected those who interacted with the individual and will affect people long after the individual has left the scene. It is the undiluted perception people have of the individual and hold to be true.

Ted Turner, the founder of CNN, was born on November 19th, 1938. At the tender age of ten, he had begun showing signs of interest in entrepreneurship. He teamed up with his father to run the unprofitable billboard business, Turner Outdoor Advertising. Through this business, Ted began to shape his legacy as one who was keen on entrepreneurship and would do whatever it took to get to the top. He also liked that his father was a devoted environmentalist – a man who was eager to protect the freshness of the air, keep trees from being decimated, and the streams from being polluted. That is what shaped Ted in early life.

In 1963, when his father, worried about the times and his failing business, committed suicide, Ted inherited the business, aware of the challenges it was facing. He had watched it grow and flounder – and was aware it had taken his father's life. It was an experience bound to affect the young Ted and cause him to think about life a certain way. His legacy began to shape with that collapsed business and his father's tragic death.

Unlike his father, though, he imagined a world in which aggressive advertising was not merely a billboard phenomenon; it was a screen affair as well. That is how he got started in TV and later founded WTBS, which pioneered the superstation concept in TV and later became TBS. Today, Ted is regarded as a leading American proprietor, producer, and philanthropist par excellence.

The Atlanta, Georgia native's most innovative and enduring legacy, perhaps, is founding a cable news network that would cover world affairs in real-time and break them on a twenty-four-hour basis. That thinking is what gave birth to CNN and has been adopted by several other networks since. No one can talk about Turner's inspiring legacy without mentioning his exploits in this field.

Notably, as a philanthropist, Ted has donated one billion dollars to support initiatives of the United Nations. This is the gift the global body used to roll out a charitable foundation to support environmental causes and other notable interests.

Therefore, legacy is not definable without going way back into the circumstances that shaped who one became. Had Ted not shown any inclination to entrepreneurship, had his father not exposed him to the need to protect the environment, and had he not encountered the tragedy of a father's suicide at an early age, he probably would have never turned out the way he did. Those early definers of life for him shaped him into the cable mogul he became and, of course, began the process of shaping up a legacy the world has joyfully celebrated.

In a world where information moves at the speed of light and changes are so frequent, is it possible to be so focused on legacy while making all the critical decisions today? Can one possibly have an image of how people will judge them ten years from today in mind as they execute their office roles? In building a legacy, there are several factors one must consider:

a. Words. Words matter a lot. In the 2020 American election, the world witnessed the impact of words. President Donald Trump started his run on the grim basis of baseless allegations about Obama's birthplace, claiming it was Africa rather than Hawaii. It was a lie followed with a slew of other lies and vitriol of a kind the USA has never seen. His corrosive words will cement his dark legacy as anchored by xenophobia and division, having been voted out of office. On the other hand, President-elect Joe R. Biden gave a victory speech that called the nation back to a unity of purpose and *civility*. When history looks back at Biden's words, they will be regarded as a key measure of his legacy and character.

b. Decisions. Decisions do matter as much as words do. One of any leader's core roles is to make decisions and live with them. The decisions a leader makes affect lives. In the USA, being the sole superpower, the decisions made in the Situation Room may affect the whole of *humanity*. Decisions made on Downing Street affect millions of people in Great Britain and the expansive Commonwealth. It is how those *impactful* decisions affect people – the effect they have on real lives – that will be regarded as one's evident legacy. We cannot talk, for example, about Margaret Thatcher's legacy without talking about the Falklands War. The war's impact on real people has been regarded as a notable aspect of Thatcher's legacy.

c. Actions. If the words and decisions of a leader matter, actions matter even more. The way a leader acts must reflect the words they speak and decisions they make. For all his claims that his policies worked for black America, the *devastation* that segment of the populace faced under Donald Trump is the real story behind his character. The actions leaders in business take and their impact on climate change, the environment, quality of life, and expansion of opportunities define their true legacy. Jack Ma and Elon Musk can only be judged based on the impact their actions as entrepreneurs have had on people's lives. Biden's legacy will be shaped by the perception of how his legacy will affect people's lives. Actions do matter, for they generate the atmosphere in which people will operate and live.

d. Treatment of people. Beyond words and decisions, and actions, a leader's core legacy is shaped by how they relate to others. Kindness, generosity, respect, and empathy go a long way in demonstrating the kind of leader one is. While it is true that not every leader can talk like Obama or be empathetic like Biden or be as charming as Bill Clinton or be as gracious as Mandela, leaders have to demonstrate care for the people they lead. How a leader engages with those they lead is, perhaps, the greatest stone laid on the foundation of their legacy.

The discussion we have just had inevitably opens the door to a fundamental question – can legacy, thus, be shaped later in one's life? Can a leader who acted in one way engineer actions that will change perceptions about themself and replace a wounded legacy with a more endearing one? This is an important question. It lies at the heart of the matter of procrastination and the delusion that one will always have time to shape a legacy.

Changing Circumstances

The curious notion that a leader can shape a legacy after leaving office has gained traction in recent years. It is propelled by those who allege that the changing nature of the times will make their words and actions be viewed differently from how they were initially perceived. The proponents of this view fail to consider that legacy is a factor of character. It begins to be shaped at birth!

Let us work with two critical examples to illustrate the point I have made about character as a central factor in shaping a legacy.

a. Martin Luther King Jr. The erroneous claim that his legacy has shifted to a more *positive* view is based on the belief that time has since smoothened the rough edges of his earlier view as a communist and terrorist – as the US government once regarded him. In reality, what has happened is that the American public has belatedly caught up to the vision he had of a unified nation guided by justice for all and opportunities based on an individual's character, not the color of one's skin. This means that Dr. King's legacy has always been anchored not on the shifting nature of politics and the times but the strength of his vision and character. Time did not *smoothen* his legacy; time vindicated him!

b. Jimmy Carter. He was a one-term president in the United States of America. His failure to deal with the Iranian Ayatollah, who had captured several service members and had occupied the American embassy in Tehran, was viewed as an act of weakness and cowardice. Carter did not want to start a war in the volatile Middle East. In 1984, though, he joined the humanitarian outfit Habitat for Humanity, an outfit founded by Millard and Linda Fuller in 1976, and improved lives around the world through the creation of decent housing. Thus, Carter went from being regarded as a failed and weak former president to a deeply admired world leader. His legacy of compassion has so dominated the perception of him that when a child was once asked what he wanted to be when he grew up, he said, "I want to be a former president, like Jimmy Carter." Yes, a legacy can shift, but only because a clear character evidenced earlier in life is the basis upon which it rests. Carter's abhorrence of war and love of humanity, which was once regarded as a minus, has become a plus in the context of being his brother's keeper!

These two examples illustrate that the passing of time does *not* change a legacy; it only clarifies it. What this means is radical – *a legacy is never changeable; it is what it is.* It is shaped as one grows up, goes to school, marries, goes to work, and eventually retires. The time to shape a legacy, therefore, is when one is in active living.

There are, however, ways one may seek to put into context their thought processes when they were in leadership. Such clarification may move the needle in the direction of a better understanding of the past and its context, but it will not change the tone of the legacy one has left behind. That said, the most dominant methods retired leaders have used to contextualize their times are:

a. Presidential Library. Recent leaders in the USA have erected large monuments in the form of presidential libraries to tell the story of their rise to the top and how they governed. Apart from creating a body of work researchers and historians can rely on to study the impact of a presidency on the world order and national politics, such edifices play the role of clarifying issues and may even change certain perceptions of the leader in question. For example, Bill Clinton has changed some perceptions of him as an ego-driven leader through his presidential library in Little Rock, Arkansas. George W. Bush has changed some perceptions of him as a clueless son of privilege through the presidential library in Dallas, Texas. Not all of us have that privilege to erect a library of such magnitude, but we can deploy other means to clarify our past actions.

b. Books. Once again, leaders have used *books* to tell the story of their life. Tony Blair and Margaret Thatcher told powerful stories in their memoirs. In America, writing to shape thought has been a hallmark of anchoring a legacy. Barack Obama wrote his memoir titled *A Promised Land*. George W. Bush wrote his, titled *Decision Points*. The former National Security Adviser, Dr. Condoleezza Rice, penned *A Memoir of My Extraordinary, Ordinary Family and Me*. These books serve to bring us into the world they lived in and explain their decisions – the goal being to help us contextualize and even empathize with them.

c. Foundation. The most known foundation in the world is *probably* the Bill and Melinda Gates Foundation. It has funded hundreds of projects around the world and donated millions to humanitarian causes. Jack Ma and Oprah Winfrey have theirs, too. These foundations have also acted as a way for former American presidents to further their influence around the world by revealing a side of them with which the public may have never had an opportunity to interact. The Ford Foundation, the Clinton Foundation, and the Obama Foundation are examples of the powerful impact a foundation can have on a legacy.

d. Teaching. Several entrepreneurs have lately resorted to teaching in universities to give back to society and shape their legacies. Condoleezza Rice took a teaching position as a Senior Fellow at Stanford University and now leads the university's Hoover Institution. Here in the UK, many former public leaders have taken up positions in our universities to shape thought and legacy. It is crucial that in doing so, one does not act in the spirit of *embellishment*, and PR is meant to give an erroneous picture of the past.

Portrayals in motion pictures, documentaries, and plays can and have been used to clarify the actions and words of a leader in their prime. In the hit motion picture *Sarafina*, Mbongeni Ngema did a fantastic job of presenting the struggles of South Africans through the prism of Nelson Mandela. Even in death, the movie lives on to cement Mandela's legacy as a freedom fighter who dedicated his life to peace.

Some find the shaping of a legacy an arduous task. That it is a lifelong endeavor is something they find discouraging rather than uplifting. That once retired, one loses the ability to change perceptions proactively is even more of a distress factor than death itself. That is the reason we warn that character always matters. Right from the time one can discern right from wrong, they are thrust in the arena of legacy-shaping and will one day be judged based on a public record piled up through the years.

Peace With A Legacy

David Cameron will never change the fact that his vision of a prosperous United Kingdom, within the context of a European Union, was shot down by enraged voters, who saw a better approach to the matter in the conservatives. Bill Clinton will never change the fact that the United States Congress impeached him over lies told to hide an affair with Monica Lewinsky. Margaret Thatcher will never change the fact that her war in the Falklands brought about untold suffering on both sides of the matter. And as much as Jack Ma may have wished to have identified his talent as an entrepreneur in his native China, he did so in the USA. Those are facts of life. They cannot be changed, regardless of the power one wields.

The question we need to ask, therefore, is what are we to do with our legacy? More precisely, what are we to do with aspects of our legacy we are not too proud of? The simple answer is – *make peace with it*. What is the point of tormenting your soul over what you have no control over? Can Clinton take back the sordid affair? Can the two Bushes – the son and the father – undo the Gulf wars? Can the Virgin Atlantic boss, Richard Branson, take back his actions in space? Can Oprah Winfrey take back the *insensitive* remarks she made on beef? The point is – what is done is done and plays into an overall legacy.

The important lesson to keep in mind is a leader must not allow one misstep to become a *pronounced* definer of their legacy. One misstep is just that – a misstep. It is when missteps become overwhelming in number that a good leader needs to worry about the statement those missteps make about them. Bill Clinton appears to have made peace with his indiscretions. George W. Bush has done the same about the Iraq War. It is a mark of outstanding leadership to understand that what has been has been and cannot be changed – *live with it*.

Don't we all wish life gave us a chance to blot out an embarrassing episode from the book of life? Don't we all secretly wish history will forget our pitfalls or will never bring them up where our uplifting accomplishments are paraded? That is just a wish. It is not reality. The reality is that the good, the bad, and the ugly come together to cement a legacy. It is the duty of each leader – and each of us – to get on the right side of history by always being aware of the judgment of time when we speak, act, and in how we treat those entrusted to our care. Legacy is about perception. Acting to diminish the negatives is the beginning of shaping an inspiring one; being careless in how we relate to others is the beginning of shaping a negative one. It is not rocket science; it is a decision we make and must later live with.

In the epilogue, we draw a conclusion about the two kinds of leadership we have been examining – Alpha and Zen. In light of the discussion we have had, what leadership mode best suits the twenty-first century? Let us conclude the matter.

EPILOGUE

The title of this book, fittingly, is *From Alpha to Zen*. In this book, you have read elements designed to move one from the realm of an Alpha leader to a Zen leader. This, therefore, is the point at which we need to ask what the title really means. Who is an Alpha leader, and who is a Zen leader? Why might a Zen leader be better than an Alpha leader?

By Alpha, what we mean is leadership defined by an acute lack of introspection, thoughtfulness, and planning. It is bereft of calmness and a discernible vision. The Alpha leader is characterized by a need to be adored, worshiped, and made to feel powerful and important. Most third-world nations are breeding grounds for this kind of leader.

On the other hand, a Zen leader is one given to thoughtfulness, introspection, and the great desire to progress along an explainable path. Such a leader only makes decisions and executes them after research, data analysis, and experts have given word about a contemplated action's credibility. Nations with governments anchored on the tenets of democracy are breeding grounds for the Zen leader and are proud of it.

The Donald Trump Presidency

It would be a massive disservice to this discussion if we failed to bring up the Trump presidency in the United States of America as an Alpha leadership example. It is not only an example of Alpha leadership but of one left untethered and unchecked.

When asked, supporters of Donald Trump would say that his most admirable qualities are confidence in his own beliefs, an egotistical and unrelenting nature, and patriotism. All these qualities led him to deliver for the American people, the lowest unemployment in seventeen years, peace to the Middle East and Operation Warp Speed. What they are unlikely to highlight, is the masterful way in which he plays the game to suit his own agenda.

From the time the far-right candidate took office, after peddling falsehoods about his predecessor's birthplace, he has acted strictly outside of established norms, showing absolute four for institutions, and acting as if he were above the law.

In just about every matter of international concern, the United States president has acted unilaterally, pulling America out of trade treaties, the World Health Organization, pulling U.S. troops out of Germany, walking away from climate-regulating pacts, and threatening to exit NATO. All these unilateral decisions have been effected without the benefit of thought or consideration for the impact on humanity.

Viewed as a reaction against globalization and pushback on President Barack Obama's dalliance with global integration of commerce, which Trump supporters regard as detrimental to their interests, the visceral response has created a vacuum in global leadership as America looked inward. Fueled by the slogan, *Make America Great Again*, the move to pull America out of world institutions, treaties, and trade pacts have all but left America standing alone at a time other world powers are jostling to replace her as the world power. China and Russia have not been too unhappy about the Alpha leadership that has characterized America over the past four years. Their only fear, if any, is the unpredictability of the man with his finger on the nation's nuclear button. That he could spark a nuclear war is the doomsday scenario world powers have been worried about.

So disruptive and chaotic has the Trump White House been that rising racial tensions, reaction to a pandemic, economic meltdown, and unilateralism have reached their peak. At the time of writing this book, Trump's Alpha leadership had just faced a resounding defeat at the polls as weary Americans turned to the genteel Joe Robinette Biden, a former vice president and senator from the state of Delaware, to steady the ship of state again.

Once again, rather than consider the impact of his actions, by creating a firestorm about irregularities allegedly committed to defraud him of victory, the Alpha leader doubled down and gave the nation a black eye in the international community, where America has been regarded as a custodian of global democracy and free-market economics. The raw calculations that drive his decision-making are on the verge of destroying an orderly transition of power to his successor when the nation is in the middle of a fight to contain a pandemic and pull back an economy ravaged by mismanagement at the federal level. His is a dictatorship in all but name, and it has scared progressive Americans.

Yet if the American people had hoped that Trump and his unpredictability would end as the nation inched closer to the inauguration of Joe Biden, they were in for a rude awakening. His team mounted one legal challenge after another in state courts and later at the Supreme Court against certification of the results. To his utter amazement, his appeals were shot down by every court, with some of the most scathing rulings having been written by the very judges he had nominated to the Ninth Circuit and the Supreme Court. He had simply decided that he was not going to accept defeat.

What many were later to discover, was that the impact of Trump's harsh rhetoric and denial of the reality of his resounding loss to Joe Biden was generating deep resentment among his far-right supporters. They viewed the loss as evidence of their growing fear that America was increasingly becoming a nation where white influence was waning at a time Latinos, Blacks and Asian-Americans were becoming more influential. The loss of Georgia and Arizona, and the gains made in Texas by the Democrats confirmed the fears of the far-right that they were steadily becoming a minority in a land in which they once were the majority. Their hope that Trump – by building a preventive wall along the southern border – was to end or dramatically scale back unchecked immigration had with his defeat come to a sudden halt.

Unnerved by this stunning loss and eager to cling on to any semblance of hope, Trump's vanquished supporters hung on to his every word, ready to hear any word that restored their faith in a process that the president had characterized as rigged and unfair. What they heard, instead, were words that called them to action, to take back their country.

The shrill rhetoric culminated with the gathering in D.C., at the National Mall, where Trump urged his supporters to go to the U.S. Capitol and take back their country from the Democrats and radical left groups. Radicalized and ready to do what they'd been charged to, Trump's supporters marched to the Capitol and stormed it, chanting to the effect that Vice President, Mike Pence, needed to be killed and Nancy Pelosi, the House Speaker, needed to be arrested. Caught flatfooted, Capitol police were overpowered and watched in disbelief as the Congress and the Senate were violated by an angry mob that clamored for the blood of leaders and proceeded to desecrate the sanctity of the secular temple of American democracy.

It took the networks some time to figure out what had happened, and once they had, they called it for what it was – an attempted coup. It had been seen in many capitals abroad, where a dictatorial leader had refused to hand over power after losing an election. And just as had happened in those foreign nations, the insurrection at the U.S. Capitol had left people dead. A police officer and four insurrectionists had been killed.

Trump read the failed insurrection as his final and most credible attempt at overthrowing the system of governance he had come to loath. Condemned by allies within and without the United States, he became so furious. He viewed the action that social media networks like Facebook, Twitter, and Google had taken to pull down his accounts as an affront to his dignity.

Trump's actions, clearly orchestrated by a certain ideological mode of consciousness and a desire to end multiculturalism in the United States, so infuriated progressives in the United States that within a, the Democrats in Congress brought to the Floor a single article of impeachment – incitement to insurrection – and impeached Trump second time; the only American president in history to have faced such humiliation. His first impeachment was for the *Abuse of Power and Obstruction of Congress* in which he was accused of having tried to influence the President of Ukraine to investigate his democratic rival for the presidency of the United States, Joe Biden.

The net impact of Trump's Alpha leadership in the United States is that it has left Americans deeply divided, isolated on the world stage, and concerned about the future of their democracy, for as one of their former statesmen once warned, "The founders gave us democracy, if we can keep it." It has taken Trump's vociferous challenge of the very tenets of that democracy for Americans to realize just how fragile democracy can be and how easily a nation can slide fully into full Alpha leadership style.

I will draw contrast to Trump's Alpha leadership by giving a brief history of Barack Obama's Zen leadership. Meanwhile, it is important for us to ask the question – what defines an Alpha leadership? What makes an Alpha leader different from a Zen leader? Going by what we have said about Donald Trump, it is easy to draw certain conclusions:

a. Strongman tendencies. Dictators are the quintessential Alpha leaders. They are free of moral boundaries, institutional checks, and operate based on lackeys who sing their thoughtless tune at every turn. In a previous chapter, we mentioned that military juntas, secretive hermit kingdoms, *hereditary* leaderships, and *pseudo* democracies are all led by Alpha males. They are a top-down leadership where only one voice is heard – the voice of the egocentric leader.

b. Disdain for facts. For a nation known for its leadership in technology, soaring medical breakthroughs, and experimentation with artificial intelligence, the despicable manner Trump has gone about dismissing health experts during a global pandemic has left the world aghast. Once again, as an Alpha leader, he is not to be disturbed by the isms and opinions of the elite men and women he regards as too smart for their own good. Facts, data, and research findings are not to find grace at his table of decision-making.

c. Lashing out. Alpha leaders are loath to any form of opposition. They cannot stand a voice that runs contrary to theirs. If anyone seeks to find out why Trump has been so angry and bitter and full of drama, look no further than the fact that he has been frustrated by the opposition directed at him by a vibrant Democratic Party and fringes in the GOP who are opposed to his style of leadership.

d. Given to frenzy. That Donald Trump still talks about crowds at his inaugural in 2016 is evidence of an Alpha leadership. Leaders of that nature are fueled by frenzy and crowds that sing their praises. At campaign rallies, a leader stuck in an Alpha mode utters words, promises, and allegations not based in the realm of facts or reason.

The net impact of an Alpha leadership is that core relations falter, and key programs get run down, morale and innovation suffer, and eventually, an enterprise implodes under the weight of mismanagement and an inability to remain competitive. In a word, what Trump has given America is – *decay*.

The Barack Obama Presidency

In 1994, he exploded on the world stage when he gave a stirring speech at the Democratic National Convention, held in Boston, Massachusetts. He was a junior senator from Illinois then. Prior to that, he had traveled to his native Kenya to trace his roots and find closure about aspects of his life that had not made sense just yet. In that search for rootedness, Barack discovered that he was a son of a deeply mixed heritage as the scion of an African father and a Caucasian mother – and had both a stepbrother and stepsister of Asian roots.

Barack was to use those racial variables to his advantage later when he ran for president of the USA. But it was the way he governed, once in that office, that is the matter we need to focus on. Barack's was an example of Zen leadership. He made his decisions only after he had carefully and widely canvassed an issue among experts. He relied on science and data and analysis to decide which way an issue was to be dealt with. He had empathy, which was exemplified by the day he showed up in Alabama to eulogize a bishop who had been killed by a white supremacist. His desire to expand healthcare to all Americans through the Affordable Care Act spoke of his thoughtfulness.

In the two terms that he served as the nation's first African-American president, Barack presided over an expanding economy, racial healing, improved relations with world powers, stronger trade treaties, and held a firm line against North Korea. Because of his evident thoughtfulness and core character, he became regarded as, perhaps, one of America's best presidents ever. That his vice president, Joe Biden, has now been elected after the chaotic and dehumanizing presidency of Donald Trump, is a matter that must be intrinsically tied to nostalgia for the calm and reason of the Obama years.

The way Obama governed is in stark contrast to the way Trump governed. Whereas Trump gave it an *Alpha* approach, Obama gave it a *Zen* approach. So, just like we extrapolated the character of Alpha leadership from Trump's disruptive and defeatist ways, we need to identify the clear nature of Zen leadership from Obama's:

    a. Participatory. Unlike in Alpha leadership, where one man or woman makes all decisions, participation is spread out in Zen leadership. Decisions are made after comprehensive consultations with experts and various stakeholders. The goal is to *share* ownership of all the successes and failures of a decision. This leads to:

- Improved worker morale.
- Self-worth among participants.
- Higher productivity.
- Soaring profits and dividends.

b. All-inclusive. By its nature, Zen leadership is thoughtful leadership. It brings people of all races, religions, social classes, and tribes together. It does not exclude others just because they are different in one way or the other. The Democratic Party, in the USA, by its nature, can only be led by a Zen leader – because of its platform based on inclusivity and tolerance for all. The Republican Party, on the other hand, is not averse to Alpha leadership because of its nature of racial intolerance and hegemony.

c. Science and Fact matter. A Zen leader is a man or woman keen on science, fact, and data. They act only after a rigorous and open-minded debate of the issues at hand. The decisions made are based purely on the conclusions drawn from data, facts, and experts' *input*. The coronavirus pandemic has demonstrated to the world how critical it is for the world to have Zen leadership at the top in powerful political capitals, at

161

the WHO, at the IMF, the World Bank, and at the Vatican. Leadership that considers the feelings of those they lead is what the twenty-first-century world craves.

d. Devoid of frenzy. Zen leadership is rested on reason, not frenzy. During the transition period between Biden and Trump, it soon became apparent that Trump and his team were not eager to transfer power smoothly. They declined to approve funds for the transition and even parted with tradition by refusing to recognize Joe Biden as the winner of the election – choosing, instead, to whip into a frenzy, supporters of the outgoing president. By contrast, Joe Biden played it cool and saw in the American institution's pillars that would withstand the grim assault on the nation's values concerning democracy.

Therefore, the question one may ask is – which of the two forms of leadership is appropriate or more effective in the twenty-first century? Is there room left for Alpha leadership anywhere in the world? Is there room left for patently autocratic approaches to leadership in global corporations and national entities? Has Zen leadership won the race?

This book has been written to present the two approaches before you and invite you to decide which feels suitable for a rapidly transforming world, where technology, medical breakthroughs, and exploration of new frontiers like space and marine life are a new reality. The collapsing borders of nations, aided in part by the social media and international networks, has also moved us in the direction of a global village.

The net impact of it all is that leaders in this *century* must adapt to a set of circumstances their older counterparts never had to. Increasingly, we will witness the evolution to Zen leadership in nations, corporations, organizations, churches, and businesses around the world. Alpha leadership, with its xenophobia, authoritarianism, lack of core inclusivity, and harmony, will be left behind as the world's mixed-race populations grow, as projected, to become a majority by 2050.

The five words that should remain in our minds as we close this book are:

- Participative.
- Tolerance.
- Science (facts, data, analysis).
- Thoughtfulness.
- Inclusivity.

Those five words are descriptive of Zen leadership. Whether we are talking about Nelson Mandela, Jack Ma, Jacinda Arden, Oprah Winfrey, Mahatma Gandhi, or any of the world's top leaders in any field, the constant is Zen Leadership. The world has steadily drifted away from Alpha leadership because it no longer serves the sensibilities of an educated, modern, and deeply sophisticated global populace.

Printed in Great Britain
by Amazon